Also by Doreen Rappaport

Be the Judge • Be the Jury
TINKER VS. DES MOINES
Student Rights on Trial

Be the Judge • Be the Jury
THE LIZZIE BORDEN TRIAL

Be the Judge • Be the Jury
THE SACCO-VANZETTI TRIAL

LIVING DANGEROUSLY
American Women Who Risked Their Lives for Adventure

ESCAPE FROM SLAVERY
Five Journeys to Freedom

AMERICAN WOMEN
Their Lives in Their Words

THE BOSTON COFFEE PARTY

TROUBLE AT THE MINES

BE THE JUDGE ? BE THE JURY™

THE ALGER HISS TRIAL

DOREEN RAPPAPORT

ILLUSTRATED WITH
PHOTOGRAPHS, PRINTS,
AND DIAGRAMS

HarperCollins*Publishers*

Grateful acknowledgment is made to the following for the use of photographs in this book: AP/Wide World Photos: 11, 42, 116. The Harvard Law School Library: 52, 107. New York *Daily Mirror*: 24. *New York Journal American*: 29, 163. The New York Public Library: 46, 48, 56, 75, 92, 98, 100, 102, 112, 118, 120, 122. *Perjury: The Hiss-Chambers Case:* 64, 79, 80, 84, 90. UPI/Bettman News Photos: 12, 15, 16, 19, 22, 31, 35, 70, 128. *The Washington Post:* 54, 83, 111, 129, 133, 134.

The Alger Hiss Trial

For information address HarperCollins Children's Books, a division of HarperCollins Publishers, 10 East 53rd Street, New York, NY 10022.

Library of Congress Cataloging-in-Publication Data
Rappaport, Doreen.
    The Alger Hiss trial / Doreen Rappaport ; illustrated with photographs, prints, and diagrams.
        p.   cm. — (Be the judge/be the jury)
    Includes bibliographical references and index.
    Summary: A reconstruction of the Alger Hiss trial, using testimony from edited transcripts of the trial, during which the reader can assume the role of juror.
    ISBN 0-06-025119-0. — ISBN 0-06-025120-4 (lib. bdg.)
    1. Hiss, Alger—Trials, litigation, etc.—Juvenile literature.   2. Trials (Perjury)—New York (N.Y.)—Juvenile literature.   [1. Hiss, Alger—Trials, litigation, etc.   2. Trials (Perjury)]   I. Series: Rappaport, Doreen. Be the judge/be the jury.
KF224.H57R36   1993   92-46155
345.747'10234—dc20   CIP
[347.47105234]   AC

1   2   3   4   5   6   7   8   9   10
❖
First Edition

For Katherine Brown Tegen,
who understands before the words are written.

Contents

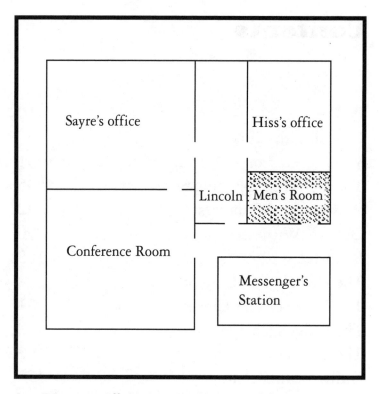

State Department offices where alleged stealing of documents took place

Everything in this book really happened. This book contains the actual testimony of the witnesses at the Alger Hiss trial.

Before the Trial

The Accusations

In August 1948 Whittaker Chambers, an ex-Communist, accused Alger Hiss, a highly respected government official, of having been a Communist spy. Hiss swore that he had never been a spy. He said he knew Chambers briefly under another name but had not seen him since July 1936. In December a federal grand jury indicted Hiss for perjury—for lying about being a spy and lying about his relationship with Chambers. The trial resulted in a "hung jury"—the jury couldn't reach a verdict. On November 17, 1949, a second trial began.

For as long as it takes you to read this book, you will BE THE JURY at the second trial. You will sit in the jury box and listen to witnesses testify and be cross-examined. You will evalu-

ate the evidence and decide whether or not Hiss
was telling the truth.

Read carefully. Think carefully about everything you read. Do not make your decision
lightly, for Alger Hiss's future is in your hands.

Who Was Alger Hiss?

As a young man, Hiss at-
tended Johns Hopkins
University on scholarship
and graduated with hon-
ors. He went on scholar-
ship to Harvard Law
School and was an out-
standing student there,
too. He served as a law clerk for Supreme Court
Justice Oliver Wendell Holmes. From 1930 to
1933 he practiced law in Boston and New
York. From 1934 to 1947 he held important
jobs in the federal government. When Chambers accused Hiss of having been a spy, Hiss
was the president of the Carnegie Endowment
for Peace. At the time of the trial forty-four-
year-old Hiss was married and lived in Washington, D.C., with his wife, Priscilla, and his
eight-year-old son, Tony.

Who Was Whittaker Chambers?

Chambers attended Columbia University in New York City for three years, where he was the editor of a literary magazine. In his junior year he joined the Communist party. In 1927 he became an editor of the Communist newspaper, *The Daily Worker*. He left the Communist party in 1929, but in 1934 he rejoined and began work as an underground agent gathering intelligence. He defected from communism again in 1938 and went to work for *Time* magazine. Eventually he became a highly respected editor and writer and an anticommunist crusader. At the time of the trial, forty-eight-year-old Chambers lived in Westminster, Maryland, on a farm with his wife, Esther, and their two children, sixteen-year-old Ellen and thirteen-year-old John.

How Did Americans Feel About Communism in 1948?

The United States fought as allies with the Soviet Union (Russia) in World War II. But soon after the war ended in 1945, Russia and the United States were engaged in a "cold war"—a war without guns.

Americans had had strong anticommunist feelings since the turn of the century. They feared communism, which was the political system in the Soviet Union. They feared that the U.S.S.R. might eventually take over the world.

In 1947 newspapers carried accusations that there were Communists in the government. The FBI investigated these accusations. Security checks were done on government workers. A loyalty oath was required of many public officials: People had to swear that they were loyal to the United States to keep their jobs. Labor unions were charged with having communists in leadership positions.

In 1947 a Congressional committee called the House Un-American Activities Committee (HUAC) held hearings on politically "subversive" people in the theater and movies. Writers, directors, and actors were called to testify. Their names were splashed across newspaper headlines. Many people denied being Communists. Some said they weren't Communists but gave names of those who were. Some people refused to testify; they said their political beliefs were none of the government's business. They were sent to jail. Many film people found their professional lives ruined. They were put on a "blacklist" and couldn't get jobs in Hollywood.

Some Americans thought the hearings were more like trials than investigations. They thought HUAC's real intention was to punish people who were critical of government policies. They thought a furious anticommunist paranoia had taken hold in the United States.

How Did Alger Hiss Get to Trial?

In July 1948 HUAC held hearings about Communists in the federal government. Elizabeth Bentley, a former Communist spy, accused top people in the government of giving her secret documents. President Harry S Truman said her accusations were false. He accused the Republicans of using the hearings to disgrace his administration.

On August 3, 1948, Whittaker Chambers testified that Alger Hiss was one of many Communists who had worked for the federal government. But, he added, none of these men had been spies.

Chambers at HUAC hearing

Hiss at HUAC hearing

On August 5 Hiss testified: "I am not and never have been a member of the Communist party. To the best of my knowledge, none of my friends is a Communist. To the best of my knowledge I never heard of Whittaker Chambers until 1947, when two FBI men asked me if I knew him. I said then I did not know him. So far as I know, I have never laid eyes on him."

Hiss was calm and relaxed as he spoke. Most reporters thought his dignified manner showed how absurd the charges were and that the committee owed him an apology. Most HUAC members wanted the investigation dropped because it was making HUAC look bad. But Richard Nixon, a first-time Republican representative from California, and Robert Stripling, HUAC's chief investigator, pressed to continue. Nixon took over the investigation.

On August 7 Chambers was re-called and offered many details to prove that he had known Hiss intimately. He said that Hiss was called "Hilly" by his wife and that Hiss called her "Dilly" or "Pross." Hiss knew Chambers by another name, "Carl." Hiss had once seen a rare bird, the prothonotary warbler. The committee members knew Chambers could have gotten some of this information from research, easily available at *Time*, but this last detail seemed too personal to have been gotten from research alone.

Richard Nixon was ambitious. He knew this case could bolster his reputation. He was determined to find out if Chambers really knew Hiss. Nixon and Stripling went twice to talk privately with Chambers at his farm.

On August 16, Hiss was re-called to a closed session. Again he denied knowing Chambers or a man named Carl. He said he had once met a writer named George Crosley and let him sublease his apartment and sold him his car. When questioned about seeing a prothonotary warbler, Hiss said he had once seen one. Hiss asked to confront Chambers.

The next day the two men were brought

together. When Hiss was asked if he had ever seen Chambers, he hesitated. He said he couldn't be sure. Chambers looked different from the man he remembered as Crosley thirteen years ago. Chambers had been heavier then. His hairline had receded. And his teeth had been fixed. Hiss asked Chambers to open his mouth wide. Hiss said Crosley had had very bad teeth. Chambers said his teeth had been fixed. Hiss asked Chambers to read from a newspaper. Then Hiss said, "The voice sounds a little less resonant than the voice I remember as George Crosley's. The teeth look improved. I am not prepared without further checking to take an absolute oath that he must be George Crosley."

Chambers said he had never used the name Crosley. He insisted he had stayed at Hiss's apartment in 1935. Hiss had given it to him for free because they were both Communists.

In the next few days the committee called many other witnesses. There were newspaper headlines and long stories about Chambers's accusations against Hiss. On August 25 television cameras crowded the hearing room. At one point, during Chambers's testimony, Hiss got so angry that he rose and walked toward him. "I challenge you," Hiss said, "to make these same statements outside of this room. And I hope you will do it damned quickly." A HUAC staff member reached his arm out to hold Hiss back. "I am not going to touch him," Hiss snapped. The man asked Hiss to sit. "I will sit when the chairman asks me," Hiss said sharply. He finally sat down, saying, "You know who started this."

Hiss had challenged Chambers to make his charges outside the hearing room because when people testify before Congress or any of its committees, they are protected from being sued even if they lie about another person. But if you say something that harms or damages the reputation of another person when you are not under

Hiss confronts Chambers

Congressional protection, that person may sue you for slander.

On August 27 Chambers was interviewed on radio. When asked whether Hiss was ever a Communist, he answered, "Alger Hiss was a Communist and may be one now." When Chambers was asked if Hiss had ever spied for the Soviets, he said, "No."

Preliminary Hearings for the Slander Trial: November 1948

Hiss filed a slander suit against Chambers, suing him for $75,000. His lawyers challenged Chambers for proof that Hiss was a Communist.

On November 17, 1948, Chambers produced typewritten copies and summaries of State Department cables and coded reports and four notes in Hiss's handwriting. Chambers said that Hiss had given him the documents. When questioned why he had previously denied that Hiss was a spy, Chambers explained that he had not wanted to inflict injury on Alger Hiss. "The Hisses had been my closest friends in the party. But now I see that Hiss is determined to destroy me and my wife, if possible."

Hiss was shocked and denied that he had stolen the documents. Chambers's lawyers turned them over to the federal authorities.

At the Chamberses' Farm: December 2, 1948

At 10:30 P.M. Chambers led two HUAC investigators to a pumpkin patch on his farm. There he opened a hollowed-out pumpkin and pulled out five rolls of microfilm. Three undeveloped rolls proved too light-struck to show anything. But two rolls of developed film contained photographs of State Department documents, three with the initials of Alger Hiss on them. Chambers said he had hidden the microfilm in the pumpkin because he thought Hiss's investigators would never find it there. The next morning Americans read about the "Pumpkin Papers,"

as this micro-film was called, in their news-papers. Nixon called a press conference. He held up a roll of microfilm and said, "It is no longer one man's word against

Richard Nixon (right) examines the microfilm

another's. Our hearings will prove to the American people once and for all that when you have a Communist, you have an espionage agent." Nixon called for Hiss's indictment.

The Grand Jury:
December 15, 1948

Chambers testified that Hiss was a Communist and had passed him government documents from 1934 to 1938. He showed copies of the stolen documents. Hiss denied the charges.

Many other people testified. The grand jury decided there was enough evidence to indict Hiss for perjury—lying under oath. Hiss could not be indicted for spying because the statute of limitations for those charges was ten years and so had run out.

HISS INDICTED ON PERJURY CHARGE

Headline from the New York *Daily Mirror*

The First Trial:
May 31, 1949–July 8, 1949

After six weeks of hearing evidence, the jury could not reach a unanimous decision. A new trial was set for November 17, 1949.

Who Took Part in This Trial?

Judge
Henry W. Goddard

Clerk

Witness Stand

12 Jurors

THE DEFENSE
Claude Cross

THE PROSECUTION
Thomas Francis Murphy

SPECTATORS

SPECTATORS

Choosing the Jury

Thursday, November 17, 1949

From the first accusations by Chambers before HUAC in August 1948, the story of Hiss's alleged espionage was headline news. During Hiss's first trial in New York City, ten officials of the American Communist party were on trial in the same courthouse for criminal conspiracy to overthrow the government. Picket lines thronged the courthouse every day. Hiss's trial had ended with a hung jury.

Now, four months later, anti-Soviet and anti-Communist feeling was even more charged. Communist rebels in China were close to gaining control of the government. In September the Soviet Union tested its first atomic bomb; many Americans were fearful now because the

United States was no longer the only nuclear power. HUAC's investigations of Soviet espionage continued.

Claude Cross, Hiss's lawyer, asked that the trial be moved to another state. This is often done when a lawyer feels his defendant cannot get a fair trial where it is scheduled to take place. The first trial judge had not been assigned to retry the case. Nixon had publicly threatened that judge with impeachment, giving the impression that the judge might have favored Hiss. Cross argued that there had been so much publicity against Hiss that it would be impossible to select twelve fair-minded jurors. The new judge turned down his request.

On Thursday, November 17, Hiss and Cross entered a courtroom packed with reporters and spectators. Alger Hiss looked dignified and handsome. His presence in court was important. What he wore, how he looked, how he carried himself or acted during the trial would affect what the jury thought of him and might affect its verdict.

A trial is like a contest between two opponents: The prosecutor represents the state; the defense lawyer represents the defendant. The contest begins with jury selection. Both sides want jurors who are impartial (unprejudiced). Among the questions the judge asked to eliminate biased jurors was, "Do you consider yourself prejudiced against testimony by Communists, ex-Communists, or those accused of Communist ties?"

Twenty-five people were excused because they had read a lot about the case. Three people were excused because they were friends of the lawyers. One man was excused because he said he couldn't possibly believe the testimony of an ex-Communist.

Within two hours, eight women and four men were chosen.

Jurors Selected For 2d Hiss Trial: Goddard Is Judge

Headline from the *New York Journal American*

The judge instructed the jurors not to talk about the case with anyone and not to read newspaper accounts about the trial. The jury was not sequestered; they were allowed to go home every night. The defense believed the jury should have been sequestered, as is often done when there has been widespread publicity about a case. The defense worried that the jury would hear and read a great deal about the case in the media and be swayed by newspaper stories that were hostile to Hiss.

The Prosecution's Opening Statement

An opening statement reviews the crime and summarizes what the prosecutor hopes to prove. Prosecutors hope their openings are effective, because they want to impress the jury even at this early moment in the trial.

Forty-three-year-old Thomas Francis Murphy was tall, with massive shoulders, long arms and legs, and a walrus mustache that covered much of his upper lip. As assistant U.S. attorney for seven years, he had prosecuted the first Hiss trial. He was determined to win the jury over this time. His deep, rumbling voice filled the courtroom.

Madame Forelady, ladies and gentlemen of the jury, you must decide if Alger Hiss lied. How do you prove that a person lies? Obviously we cannot have a film of it. We do not always have direct proof of this crime. You will decide by circumstantial evidence. You must reason and look at the facts.

Now what do we say Hiss lied about? On December 15, 1948, a grand jury questioned Hiss. We say he told two lies then. The first lie was that he did not give State Department documents to Chambers. The second lie Hiss told was that he did not see Chambers after January 1, 1937. That date is important because the stolen documents were all dated the first three months of 1938.

One of our witnesses is Whittaker Chambers. From his twenty-third birthday until he was thirty-eight, Chambers was an active paid worker of the Communist party and a spy for Russia. From 1935 until 1938, Hiss passed him stolen documents. During that time Chambers and his wife were most intimate with Hiss and his wife. Chambers will tell you what they did together and where they went. He will tell you how Hiss gave him his apartment to live in and donated a car for a Communist organizer. He will tell you that in 1937 Hiss told a Russian officer named Bykov that he would get State Department documents for the Russians.

Every two weeks, Chambers picked up documents at Hiss's house, had them microfilmed, and returned them to Hiss. After two years, the Communists wanted more documents. So each night Hiss's wife typed documents, and he returned the originals to his office the next day. Now when Chambers came every two weeks, he picked up many more papers than before.

In 1937 Chambers realized that communism was wrong. But he knew he could be killed if he left the Communist party. He did it anyway. His wife and two little children went with him into hiding with a gun, because he was afraid of what the Communists might do to him. Then he set out to earn a living honestly. After ten years of brilliant hard work, he became a senior editor of *Time*, one of our largest national magazines. He worked so hard, he had a heart attack. He rested on his farm in Maryland and then went back to work.

In August 1948 Chambers testified before the House Committee on Un-American Activities. He said that he had been a Communist and a spy. He said Hiss was a Communist, too. Hiss denied the charges. In fact he said the name Whittaker Chambers meant nothing to him. He was shown photographs of Chambers. He said he did not know him. After a few more sessions, Hiss finally identified Chambers and said he knew him under another name.

The committee members were confused. They didn't know which man to believe. On December 15, 1948, both men testified before a grand jury. The grand jury believed Chambers. They believed that Alger Hiss lied. They indicted Hiss for perjury.

The defense will make a big deal about the fact that Chambers lied many times. And he did. But they won't say that he lied when he said that Hiss was a Communist because each time he testified he said that Hiss was a Communist.

What did Chambers leave out when he testified? He lied all three times when he said no one had spied. Chambers will explain why it took him a while to say that Hiss stole the documents.

This is a very poor summary of what we intend to prove. Take the evidence from the witness chair only and decide if it proves beyond a reasonable doubt that Whittaker Chambers is telling the truth.

The Defense's Opening Statement

Fifty-six-year-old Claude Cross was an experienced lawyer from Boston. Short and stocky, with a round, chubby face, he provided a marked contrast to the six-foot prosecutor.

The prosecutor said that the grand jury believed Chambers and not Hiss. That is not evidence for this trial. The only evidence you may consider will be what you hear from the witnesses. You must decide, did Alger Hiss turn over secret documents to Whittaker Chambers? The only person who will testify that Hiss did this will be Chambers. You must decide which man lied.

Hiss was a respected lawyer and government official. Much confidential information was entrusted to him. Chambers was a Communist for at least fourteen years and was committed, if necessary, to overthrowing our government by violence. Chambers says he left the party in 1938, but there is conflicting evidence about that.

In late 1934 or early 1935, Chambers, masquerading as a writer, went to see Hiss, who was then a lawyer for a senate committee. Many journalists called Hiss for information. Hiss saw him twice in his office and at lunch three or four times. Chambers said he needed an apartment in Washington. Hiss and his wife were moving and had two months left on the lease of their old apartment. Hiss offered Chambers his old apartment for what it cost him. Chambers took it.

At that time the Hisses were buying a new car and had not yet traded in their old Ford. As part of the rental agreement, Hiss gave Chambers the old car for fifty dollars. Of course, it turned out that Chambers didn't pay the rent. He also didn't pay back some other small sums of money he borrowed from Hiss. In July 1936, Hiss decided Chambers was a deadbeat. He told him off and never saw him again. Chambers says that they saw each other after that.

Chambers said he was known to the Hisses as Carl.

The Hisses say they knew him as George Crosley. Chambers used many false names.

Hiss sued Chambers for slander. Would he have done this if he was a spy and knew that Chambers had papers in his handwriting and papers typed on his typewriter?

When the lawsuit began, Hiss's lawyers asked Chambers for proof that Hiss was a spy. Three days later he produced an envelope of stolen documents. He said he had stored them in his nephew's apartment ten years before. But his nephew did not see him open that envelope, so we only have Chambers's word that secret documents were in it.

Four of the documents are memos in Hiss's handwriting. Not the slightest question about it. How they were gotten we will never know. All the typewritten documents, except Exhibit 10, were typed on a Woodstock typewriter that once belonged to Mr. and Mrs. Hiss. As to who actually typed the documents, only the person who did it knows. The Hisses' maid and her son will testify that the Hisses gave them this typewriter in late December 1937. So Mrs. Hiss could not have typed these documents, because they were all typed after January 1, 1938.

Exhibit 10 and Document 13 were sent only to the Far Eastern Division. From March 1936 until March 1938 Julian Wadleigh in the Trade Agreements Division was stealing papers and turning them over to Chambers. We believe there was another thief in the Far Eastern Division.

When Chambers first produced the documents, he did not turn over everything he had. A few days later, he showed two FBI men microfilm that he had secreted in a hollowed-out pumpkin on his farm. The microfilm contained photographs of documents from Wadleigh's division. Three documents were dated January 14, 1938. These documents had the stamp of Hiss's boss, Francis B. Sayre, and the initials A.H.— Alger Hiss. You will learn that on the afternoon of January 14, Sayre was out of his office. Wadleigh often visited Sayre's office and stopped by Hiss's office to talk with him.

Several of these typewritten documents did not go to Sayre's office. And if they did not go to Sayre's office, they could not have been stolen by Hiss and typed by his wife, unless he stole them from some other office.

We believe that either Chambers or one of his confederates typed those documents. Any man who got people to steal top-secret documents out of the State Department wouldn't have had much trouble tracing and getting the Woodstock typewriter, wherever it was.

So, did Alger Hiss transfer documents to Chambers in 1938? You will have to decide.

Be the Jury

Now listen to the evidence and search for the truth. Remember that even though Hiss has been charged with perjury, he is still presumed to be innocent. The prosecutor does *not* have to prove Hiss guilty beyond all *possibility* of a doubt, but the prosecutor must establish his guilt beyond a *reasonable* doubt. The defense does not have to prove his innocence. The defense only needs to point out flaws in incriminating evidence to convince the jury that guilt was not proved.

What is a *reasonable* doubt? A doubt for which some reason can be given. It must come from the evidence or from the lack of evidence. It *cannot* come from the fact that there are other solutions to the crime that are believable. A doubt cannot be based on a guess or thought unrelated to the evidence. A doubt *cannot* be based on sympathy for Hiss or a belief that his acts should not be illegal, or from the jury's wish to avoid the disagreeable job of convicting him.

The Prosecution's Strategy

In trying to prove Hiss guilty of perjury beyond a reasonable doubt, the prosecutor will present evidence to establish:

- his *motive* for espionage (that he was a Communist);
- the *plan and method* to get the documents (premeditation);
- the *opportunity* to get the documents;
- the *means* to type the documents (the typewriter);
- that Hiss and Chambers had a *close association*; and
- that Hiss saw Chambers *after 1937*.

The Defense's Strategy

In trying to show the defendant not guilty beyond a reasonable doubt, the defense will cross-examine each of the prosecution's witnesses, hoping to cast doubt on their testimony. The defense will challenge whether the witness's story is accurate or believable. Sometimes the defense will try to show that the witness told a different story about the same thing at another time. The defense will also suggest other explanations for damaging testimony, which will be more fully developed when it presents its case.

Prosecution Witnesses

Thursday, November 17 and Monday, November 21, 1949
Witness: **Whittaker Chambers**
Direct Examination by the Prosecution

On the afternoon of the first day, the prosecution called its star witness to the stand. Each side presents witnesses whose testimony tends  to support its side of the case. All testimony must clearly relate to the main issue. Generally witnesses cannot give their opinions.

Whittaker Chambers was short and

overweight. Many of the reporters thought that he looked more relaxed and was better dressed than he had been at the first trial, when his suits often looked as if they needed to be pressed. He was the only witness who would testify that Hiss had been a spy. Much of his testimony was circumstantial evidence. He would testify to circumstances and the jury would draw conclusions from these circumstances. The prosecutor knew that if the jury did not believe Chambers, there was no case.

Chambers talked about his early life. He and his brother had grown up in poverty. His father left the family when he was five, and sent only eight dollars a week for their support. Chambers was a brilliant student in high school, but he felt like an outsider. He was chosen to speak at graduation, but the principal did not approve his speech. He was asked to rewrite it. He did, but at graduation he read his original speech and was disgraced. He went to Williams College for two days but left because he "thought it was too rich for his blood." He attended Columbia University, working at night at the New York Public Library at 42nd Street. One time when the library was missing books, library officials searched his locker and found Communist pamphlets. They searched his apartment and found books he had taken from Columbia University, but they didn't find any books from the public library. Chambers got into trouble at Columbia when he published a controversial play about Jesus Christ in the school paper. He dropped out of college. He became a Communist in 1925 and worked his way up from selling the Communist newspaper *The Daily Worker* to being an editor of the paper. In 1935 he joined the Communist underground. Chambers testified that he supervised two other spies along with Alger Hiss.

Q. Tell us about your relationship with Hiss.
A. In June or July 1934 I met Hiss at his apartment. I was using the alias "Carl" then. He was working for a Senate Committee and had access to confidential State Department documents. My boss, J. Peters, who was the head of the whole underground of the American Communist party, wanted those documents. So Hiss got them. Every ten days or so I picked up the documents at his house between five P.M. and six P.M., had them photographed, and returned them the same night. In 1936 Hiss was of-

fered a job in the Justice Department. I told him the party wanted him to take it. In January 1937 I took Hiss to New York City to meet Colonel Bykov. Bykov was a stocky, well-built man. He spoke to us in German. I translated. Bykov asked Hiss to get State Department documents. Hiss agreed. Bykov wanted Hiss's brother to get State Department docu-

REDS MADE HISS STATE DEPT. MAN

Headline from the New York *Daily Mirror*

ments, too. Hiss said he didn't know if his brother was developed enough for such work. Bykov suggested that Hiss persuade him.

A few months later I told Hiss we wanted more papers. So he brought the documents home and Mrs. Hiss typed them.* She had always wanted to do underground work. Sometimes Hiss gave me small handwritten notes about documents that he had seen but couldn't get out. In 1937 I gave Hiss an Oriental rug in appreciation of his work for the Russians. My friend Meyer Schapiro got me the rug. I met Hiss at

---

*Photocopying had not been invented in 1938. The common practice was to make carbon copies.

the parking lot of a restaurant on the highway to Washington and gave him the rug. I have seen this rug rolled up in a closet in Mr. Hiss's apartment. We worked together until April 1938, when I left the party.

Q. Did you see Mr. and Mrs. Hiss socially?

A. Yes. Shortly after I met Hiss, he was moving to a furnished house. I needed an apartment in Washington. Hiss offered me his old apartment for free. The day we were supposed to move in, the van with our furniture didn't come, so we stayed with the Hisses in their new place for a few days.

When we moved to New York City, they visited us in June or July 1935. It was miserably hot. Hiss showed me an ad for a cottage in Long Eddy, New York. I went with them in their Ford to see it. The cottage wasn't good. My wife and I rented a cottage in Smithtown that summer.

Hiss and his lawyer looked up in surprise.

WELL FURNISHED COTTAGES on Delaware River: mountains, fishing, bathing; improvements; $100 season. Bishop, Long Eddy. N. Y.

Chambers had never mentioned this trip to Long Eddy before.

Mrs. Hiss visited us there for ten days. I'm not sure in what part of the summer. That fall we stayed at the Hisses' home for a few days. I thought I might be going to Europe and my wife and child would stay with them. I didn't go, though.

Sometime around Christmas 1937 they visited us at our house at Mount Royal Terrace in Baltimore.

Chambers gave many other details of social times with Hiss and his wife to prove how friendly he and his wife were with them. He described in great detail the outsides and insides of their four homes. He told of gifts the Hisses had given him—a dining-room table, an armchair, and a chest of drawers. Chambers's voice was soft and flat as he gave detail after detail. He spoke calmly, and some of the reporters thought he seemed emotionally detached from his words.

Chambers described a trip to New Hampshire in August 1937. The prosecution believed this trip proved he had seen Hiss in 1937.

Q. Did you ever take any other trips together?
A. Yes. On August 9, 1937, we went to Peterborough, New Hampshire, so I could see another agent, Harry Dexter White, who was the assistant secretary of the Treasury. We drove up to White's driveway.

The Hisses waited in the car for about twenty minutes while I talked with White. Afterward we stopped at a pond and Mrs. Hiss swam. We stayed overnight at a place called Bleakhouse. The next day, we saw the play *She Stoops to Conquer* at a theater near Peterborough. Then we drove back to New York.

The prosecutor showed the jury an advertisement for the play and a photograph taken by Chambers of White's driveway.

(Advertisement)

PETERBOROUGH PLAYERS
Professional Summer Company
Stearns Farm   -   -   -   -   Middle Hancock Road

"She Stoops to Conquer" or "Mistakes of a Night"
Hilarious Comedy by Oliver Goldsmith

Beginning next Tuesday and running thru Sunday
Curtain at 8 :30 P. M., D. S. T.
Admission at Box Office $1.10 inc. tax
Phone Reservations   -   Peterborough 343

Q. Did Hiss ever give you a car?
A. Yes. He had an old Ford, and in 1936 he told me he wanted to donate it to some poor Communist organizer. I spoke to Peters. He allowed it.

Chambers explained how frightened he was to leave the Communist party and what he did to protect himself.

Q. How did you prepare to leave the party?
A. I started planning in late 1937. First I took a job with the federal government. I was afraid the Communists might kill me for leaving. I had been using false names and I thought if I started using my own name, it would be more difficult for them to kill a man with an identity. In November 1937 I told Hiss I wanted to buy a car, and he loaned me four hundred dollars. That Christmas I told Hiss that I was leaving the party. He cried when I told him. I finally left on April 15, 1938.

On many different occasions Chambers had told FBI investigators, members of HUAC, and the grand jury that he knew nothing of any spying. The prosecution wanted the jury to understand why he had lied so they would believe him now.

Q. Why did you finally testify about the spying?
A. Up until I was sued by Mr. Hiss, I didn't want to injure people involved in the Communist conspiracy. I had found the strength to break with the party and had had time to work out a new life. I wanted to give these people the same chance. But when Mr. Hiss sued me, I had no choice but to reveal these documents.

Q. How did you find your farm in Maryland?

A. I first saw it with Hiss in 1935. He put money down for it but withdrew from the deal. I bought it in 1937.

Q. Why did you put the microfilm in the pumpkin?

A. Mr. Hiss's investigators had been in and out of my farm for some time. I didn't want them to find it.

Be the Jury

Why did Hiss let someone he hardly knew stay in his apartment?

Is the photograph proof that Hiss went with Chambers to see Harry Dexter White?

Tuesday, November 22– Monday, November 28, 1949

Cross-Examination by the Defense

Q. You mentioned a brother. Did he commit suicide?
A. Yes.

The prosecutor did not want the jury to hear this information, so he exercised the right to *object* to the testimony. He said this evidence was *inadmissible* because it didn't relate to the case. The defense argued that it was important for psychiatric testimony later. When lawyers argue over evidence, the judge does not take sides. He or she listens and, based on rules about evidence, decides whether or not the evidence should be admitted. When a judge *sustains* an objection, evidence is not presented. If the objection is *overruled*, evidence is admitted.

The judge overruled the objection and allowed the testimony.

Q. Did your brother ask you to enter into a suicide pact with him?

Again the prosecutor objected and was overruled.

A. Yes.

Q. What was your relationship with your brother?

A. Before his death my mother asked me to watch over him to stop him. We became close. When he killed himself, I was almost paralyzed. I had no desire to do anything. My brother's death set a seal on my being a Communist. I was one before, but I became a fanatical one afterward. I guess I became spiritually closer to him after his death.

The defense needed to show that Chambers was too great a liar to be believed. Chambers admitted that he had used at least eleven aliases. He had used the name Breen for his passport and when he lived in Smithtown. He had changed his child's name to Ursula and his wife's name to Edna. He admitted that he had lied on his application for the government job. He admitted that when he first told about Communists in the government, he didn't say anything about Hiss meeting Bykov in New York.

Cross rapidly questioned Chambers about more inconsistencies in his story. Chambers remained calm and unruffled. Some jury members yawned, others shuffled their feet and changed their positions. Some gazed about the courtroom.

Q. You told HUAC in August 1948, and then the FBI and then the grand jury in October 1948, that you didn't know any spies. So you either lied then or now?

Chambers answered confidently:

A. That is right.

Julian Wadleigh, who worked for the Trade Agreements Division of the State Department, had passed documents to Chambers. Hiss and Wadleigh worked in the same building. Hiss worked on the second floor; Wadleigh worked on the first floor. The defense hoped to show that Wadleigh had stolen these documents, since so many of them came from his division.

Q. Did you get documents from Julian Wadleigh?
A. Yes, from about early March 1936 until early in 1938. I met him once a month, usually on the street, around 4:30 to 7 P.M. He gave me ten to twenty-five documents in a briefcase. I had the documents micro-

Chambers Describes Wadleigh Dealings

Headline from *The Washington Post*

filmed. We put a number on the left-hand upper corner so that the photographer could take the picture with a number on each page and run the numbers consecutively. I took Wadleigh to meet Bykov once.

Q. Did you ever socialize with Wadleigh and his wife?

A. No.

The defense needed to prove that Chambers lied about the trip to Peterborough.

Q. Harry Dexter White died suddenly after being questioned by HUAC. Did you ever say anything about this trip to Peterborough before he died?

A. I do not believe so.

Q. On this six-hundred-mile trip from Washington to Peterborough, did you stop to sleep?

A. Yes, we stopped in Thomaston, Connecticut, at a tourist home. But I don't remember the name.

Q. Have you tried to find this guest house?

A. Yes, I went up there twice with the FBI, but we couldn't find it.

Q. When you went to the guest house in Peterborough, did you see your name or the Hisses' names in the registry?

A. No, our names were not in the book.

Chambers claimed that Hiss lent him $400 for a car, but the defense believed he got the money from his mother.

Q. In 1937, when you bought the farm in Maryland, where did you get the $650 for it?

A. From my mother.

Q. In 1938, you bought a place in Baltimore. Where did you get the $500 down payment?

A. From my mother.

The defense moved on to the crucial question of when Chambers left the party. On at least sixteen different occasions, he had said he quit the party in 1937. If he had left the party in 1937, he could not have gotten these documents from Hiss, for they were all dated the first three months of 1938.

Through the defense's questioning it was shown that Chambers stopped using false names in 1937. He had a telephone line under his own name in later 1937, and Mrs. Chambers used her own name on her driver's license at that time. The evidence did not change Chambers's story. He admitted that he had lied before but insisted that he was not lying now: He had left the party in mid-1938.

The defense showed Chambers Exhibit 10, a report on the military situation between China and Japan. This report had not been typed on the Woodstock typewriter.

```
        Japanese are reported to be moving 80,000 fresh troops from
Japan via Mukden.  First of these troops arrived at Mukden on
December 17th.  Believes they are destined for the northern frontier
Barracks with a capacity of 50,000 troops are reported to have been
erected at Chaimussu and Poli in northeast Manchuria.  Other
barracks with capacities for 100,000 troops are reported to be
located between railroads which are rapidly being pushed to the
Mongolian and northeast frontiers.  Japanese agents are reported
to be fomenting action by Mohammedans in Ninghsia and Chenghi
to harrass the Urunchi-Lanchow Road.
```

Chambers admitted that he might not have gotten it from Hiss. The defense was surprised. Every other time he had testified, Chambers had sworn all the documents came from Hiss.

Q. But every time before this, you said all the documents came from Hiss?

A. Yes, but as I looked at it now, it occurred to me

that Exhibit 10 is the kind of stuff Harry Dexter White usually gave me.

Q. But you never told the FBI this in the three months you talked with them, five days a week, all day?

A. No.

Q. Don't documents 1 through 50 all represent papers given to you from one delivery, and weren't they all microfilmed together?

A. Yes.

Q. So if you know who gave you any of these papers, you know who gave you all the others?

A. Yes.

Tuesday, November 29, 1949
Redirect by the Prosecution

The prosecution needed to confirm that Hiss, not Wadleigh, had given Chambers these documents.

Q. How do you know Hiss gave you all the papers?

A. I have no independent memory of receiving each paper, but there is no doubt in my mind that Hiss gave me each paper. None of these documents could have come from Wadleigh, even though he was an active source, because I never received any typed papers from Wadleigh. I did receive typed copies of originals from Harry Dexter White.

Q. Did you ever show anyone the furniture you got from Hiss?

A. Yes, I showed it to Mr. McLean, one of Hiss's lawyers, when he came to my farm.

Be the Jury

Why aren't their names on the registry at Bleakhouse if they stayed there?

Why couldn't Chambers find the place in Thomaston?

If Exhibit 10 wasn't typed on Hiss's typewriter, who stole it?

Could the other documents come from Wadleigh or someone else?

Why did Chambers testify before that he left the party in 1937 if he left in 1938?

If Chambers lied so many times before, why should I believe him now?

Wednesday, November 30, 1949
Witness: Nathan Levine
Direct Examination by the Prosecution

Levine was Chambers's nephew by marriage. The prosecution believed his evidence confirmed that Chambers had hidden away the documents. Levine's testimony was *circumstantial*: He testified to circumstances surrounding the crime, and the jury drew conclusions from these circumstances.

Q. In 1938 did you receive an envelope from your uncle?

A. Yes. And I put it away for safekeeping in the top of the linen closet.

Q. When did you next see it?

A. Last year. Mr. Chambers came and I gave it to him.

Q. Had you ever looked inside this envelope?

A. No.

Cross-Examination by the Defense

The defense raised doubts that there had ever been documents in the envelope.

Q. Did you ever see the contents of the envelope?
A. No.

The defense pointed out that Chambers had lied even to his relatives.

Q. Did Mr. Chambers live with your parents?
A. Yes. In 1936 or 1937, he stayed for a few months. We didn't see him too much, though.

Q. Did you or your parents have any idea that he was a Communist or a spy?
A. No. I thought he was a translator of books.

Be the Jury

Did anyone else but Chambers see that the documents were in the envelope?

Thursday, December 1– Monday, December 5, 1949

Witness: Walter H. Anderson

Direct Examination by the Prosecution

Anderson was the chief of the Records Branch at the State Department. In a soft, patient voice, he explained that two kinds of carbon copies were made of each incoming cable. A single "action copy," made on yellow paper, became a permanent record for the files. "Information copies," on white paper, were sent to selected officials. Each document was color- and letter-coded to show how confidential it was. A record was kept of where everything went. Documents were usually picked up and burned after a week, but the records didn't specify how many were picked up and burned. The records showed that Exhibit 10 went only to the Far Eastern Division.

Huge photographic enlargements of the documents were placed on a seven-foot easel. The type was forty-nine times larger than the original size. The prosecutor read some documents aloud. Reporters wondered if the jurors found this repetition as boring and frustrating as they did.

Cross-Examination by the Defense

Anderson explained that many people in the State Department had the chance to read the information copies. Sometimes twenty-five copies of a cable were given out. During work hours the information copies were kept in unlocked cabinets. At least thirty-five people had access to the code room. Probably 250 people had access to each document. During the years 1935 to 1938 security was not that strict.

Monday, December 5, 1949
Witness: William Rosen
Direct Examination by the Prosecution

Juror's sketch*

Rosen was sixty-five years old. He was slight with gray hair and wore horn-rimmed glasses. His name appeared on the Motor Vehicle Bureau Department record as the buyer of Hiss's 1929 Ford, which Chambers said Hiss had donated for a Communist organizer.

Q. Were you in July 1936 connected with the Communist party?

A. I respectfully decline to answer this question on the grounds of the Fifth Amendment that I may incriminate myself, and on the grounds of the First Amendment that I don't have to divulge my associations.

Rosen spoke so softly, it was hard to hear him.

Q. Are you the William Rosen whose name is on the title certificate of Mr. Hiss's Ford car?

*One juror made sketches of some of the witnesses.

Rosen refused to answer that question or any other questions about whether he knew Hiss. The defense objected to his testimony because his not answering might make the jurors think he was a Communist and that he knew Hiss. The judge overruled the defense and the questioning continued.

Cross-Examination by the Defense

The defense did not want Hiss associated with a Communist.

Q. Did you ever see Mr. Hiss before this trial?
A. No.
Q. Have you ever spoken to him or dealt with him?
A. No.

The judge told the jury, "You are to draw no inference unfavorable to the defendant because this witness declined to answer any questions."

Be the Jury

Why is Rosen's name on the ownership certificate if Hiss gave the Ford to Chambers?

Could Chambers have turned the car over to Rosen without telling Hiss?

Witness: **Eunice Lincoln**
Direct Examination by the Prosecution

Lincoln was Sayre's secretary from 1933 to 1939. Her testimony emphasized how difficult it was for anyone to sneak into Sayre's or Hiss's office.

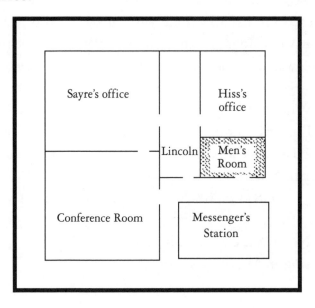

Q. Did visitors enter without talking to you?
A. No. A messenger sat outside the office. He usually opened the door and took visitors' coats and hats. I never let anyone in without asking them what they wanted. I usually announced everyone. If I knew the person, I would let him go in. Someone always

covered the office. There were two entrances to Mr. Sayre's office, but the inner one, to the room where meetings were usually held, was locked.

Q. What happened at the end of the day?

A. I took signed mail off Mr. Sayre's desk and anything that needed to be locked up. I did the same for Mr. Hiss. I locked the papers in a file cabinet. The papers were usually trade agreement telegrams and copies of things written in our office. Sometimes there was a carbon of a memo written somewhere else.

Q. What did you do with the information copies?

A. Each week I collected them after Mr. Sayre and Mr. Hiss had read them and put them in an envelope. Later they were picked up for burning.

Q. In 1938 did Mr. Wadleigh come frequently to your office?

A. No. I remember only once when he came to a meeting in Mr. Sayre's office.

Cross-Examination by the Defense

The defense needed to show that many people had access to these offices.

Q. Were there times when Mr. Sayre left his office through Room 214 and you didn't see him?

A. Yes. And then the messenger let me know.

Q. Did anyone ever share Mr. Hiss's office?

A. Yes. There was an extra desk and a typewriter there. Mr. Grady came at different times. And Mr. Dickey was there from time to time. Mr. Darlington was there too. Maybe at the same time that Mr. Wadleigh was working there.

Q. Were information copies out on the desks during the day?

A. Yes.

Q. Did some department officials include carbons along with an original memo, so Mr. Sayre could keep the carbon?

A. Yes.

Be the Jury

Could someone have gotten into these offices and stolen the documents?

Tuesday, December 6, 1949
Witness: Esther Chambers
Direct Examination by the Prosecution

Esther Chambers was short and slim with a pleasant face framed by dark hair and glasses that seemed oversized for her thin face. She answered all questions cautiously in a soft voice. She explained that she had been sympathetic toward the Communist party but had never joined. She had willingly assumed the many aliases required by her husband's underground work. She had once even changed her first name and the name of her daughter. The prosecution believed Mrs. Chambers's testimony corroborated that the two families had a close relationship.

Q. Tell us about moving into the Hisses' apartment.
A. Sometime in May or June 1935 Mr. Hiss moved our baby's crib and other things in his Ford into the apartment. We stayed there about six weeks. We didn't bring any furniture because they left us amply

supplied. During that time Alger took us and the baby for rides to Haines Point. Once we went to look at the roses in bloom. Another time we went to Mount Vernon.

Q. When did you next see the Hisses?

A. They visited us in New York. I have a mental picture of my husband and the Hisses poring over a map, looking for a place called Long Eddy. They drove there to look at a cottage. We were going to rent it with them for the summer. Instead we went to Smithtown. Mrs. Hiss visited us there for ten days. She helped me with the baby so I could have time to paint. I gave her one of my paintings. She put it up in her dining room. After Smithtown we stayed with the Hisses for five days. They moved their son's furniture into the second floor and we had the top floor. We all ate together like one family. Then we moved to Baltimore. The Hisses gave us some furniture.

Mrs. Chambers looked up at the ceiling in between questions and often blinked before answering.

Q. What did you call the Hisses?

A. I called Alger "Hilly" and so did the baby. I called Mrs. Hiss "Pross." She called me "Liza."

Q. What did the Hisses call your husband?

A. "Carl."

The Hisses had moved four times from 1935 to 1938. Mrs. Chambers testified that she had visited all four residences. She also said that the FBI men had taken her and her husband to see the outsides of all these houses and had shown her floor plans of the insides of the houses.

Mrs. Chambers said that the houses on 30th Street and Volta Place were painted white outside. She said the living room at 30th Street was pink. She gave many details about wallpapers, room colors, and furniture. She insisted she had not been inside these houses since 1938.

Q. Did you visit them at their 30th Street apartment?

A. Yes. Twice. The second visit was that New Year's Eve party my husband testified about. We drank port. That is indelibly impressed on my mind because my husband was violently sick after it.

Q. Did you visit their Volta Place house?

A. Yes, shortly after they moved in. The four of us had a little housewarming party. They served us little sandwiches that they had served that afternoon to other guests.

Mrs. Chambers noted at least twenty times she had been with the Hisses, but she couldn't give any specific dates.

Q. Did you see the Hisses in Baltimore?

A. Yes, I saw a great deal of them when we lived at Eutaw Place. We went to a few Russian films together. They ate at our house several times. Once Mrs. Hiss stayed overnight with the baby when I went to New York to the doctor. She also met me several times in the square in front of Eutaw Place.

They also visited us when we lived at Auchentoroly Terrace and then when we moved to Mount Royal Terrace. One night in December 1937 they brought a bottle of California champagne. The maid was gone and the babies were in bed. We celebrated their wedding anniversary.

Q. When did your husband leave the Communist party?

A. When we were living at Auchentoroly Terrace.

Q. Didn't you move from Auchentoroly Terrace in November 1937?

A. Yes, I think so.

Wednesday, December 7, 1949

Cross-Examination by the Defense

Mrs. Chambers's testimony from the first trial was submitted as evidence. Written records are kept of trial testimony. These records are often used to point out inconsistencies in a witness's testimony. The defense believed that the many inconsistencies in Mrs. Chambers's testimony cast doubt on her as a reliable witness.

Q. Today you testified to several incidents you never described before, such as poring over the maps and your husband driving to Long Eddy with the Hisses.

A. Yes, I didn't remember that before, so I didn't testify about it. I will probably keep remembering things for the rest of my days.

Q. Now when did this party at Mount Royal Terrace take place?

A. In the middle of December 1937.

Q. But when you testified about it at the first trial, you said it was a New Year's Eve party?

A. No, I said it was the wedding anniversary.

Mrs. Chambers answered so softly the defense repeatedly asked her to speak up.

Q. But when you testified before, you said the Hisses never came to Mount Royal.

A. Probably I didn't remember at that time.

Q. This New Year's Eve party you talked about. Was it December 1936 or December 1937?

A. I think it was 1936 but I can't be certain.

Q. In Baltimore and at the first trial you said Mrs. Hiss did not stay overnight. Did you just remember this since the last trial?

A. Yes, probably.

Q. In Smithtown did Mrs. Hiss meet your landlord?

A. Yes. He came for coffee maybe six times when she was there.

Q. This is Volta Place after a remodeling in 1946. Is this how you remember it?

Volta Place after remodeling   Sketch before remodeling

A. No, it did not look anything like that. The wall was there and the gate was there but I don't remember any iron rail or windows.

The defense read from her testimony at the first trial when she had described the concrete porch and railing in the photograph.

Mrs. Chambers nervously answered:

A. I hadn't seen this photograph before and I don't want to see it now. I regret my memory isn't better. The picture is generally the same but I don't remember the iron railing. But I just may not have noticed it.

Q. What color was the living room at 30th Street?

A. Pink.

Previous testimony was read that stated that Mr. Chambers's mother had given them money many times.

Q. Did you say she once gave you money to buy a car?

A. I think so. I am not certain. These things were taken care of by him.

Redirect by the Prosecution

Q. Is it true that during all your testimony, in Baltimore and at the first trial and now here, that you are trying to give us your best recollection of the facts?
A. Yes.

Q. When you were questioned before about buying the Ford, did you know if your mother-in-law gave you the money?
A. No. The money was given to me by my husband. I did not know then nor did I know later where it came from.

Be the Jury

If Mrs. Chambers hadn't seen Volta Place since 1938, why did she describe it as it looked after 1946?

How could Mrs. Chambers know so much about the Hisses' homes if she hadn't been there?

Why did Mrs. Chambers tell so many different versions of the same events?

When did Chambers say he left the party?

Witness: **Ramos Feehan**

Feehan, a laboratory agent for the FBI, was an expert witness. Expert witnesses are sometimes police officers or handwriting experts. Expert witnesses may interpret evidence and give opinions.

Feehan had examined the typewritten documents. He explained that all documents, except Exhibit 10, had been typed on the Hisses' Woodstock typewriter. Enlargements of the typed documents and of letters typed by Mrs. Hiss on the Woodstock stood on two easels. Feehan stood on a platform and used a pointer to show similarities and convince the jury that the stolen documents had been typed on the Hisses' typewriter.

Witness: **Meyer Schapiro**

Schapiro, a professor of art at Columbia University, knew Chambers from college. He testified that in December 1936 Chambers had asked him to get four Oriental rugs. A receipt for the four rugs was submitted as evidence. The rugs were shipped to Washington, D.C., to a man named Silverman.

The defense declined to cross-examine Schapiro.

Thursday, December 8– Friday, December 9, 1949

Witness: **Julian Wadleigh**

Direct Examination by the Prosecution

Wadleigh was a slim, brown-haired man with horn-rimmed glasses. He spoke with an accent that he had acquired when he studied economics in England at Oxford University and the University of London. Wadleigh claimed that from late 1935 to March 1938, he passed to Chambers documents from his department. He never became an official member of the party; he called himself a voluntary collaborator. He said he turned over documents to the Soviets because they were the only world power at that time actively against Hitler and Nazi Germany.

One at a time, the prosecutor handed Wadleigh each of the forty-seven documents and asked:

Q. Did you ever give these to Chambers?

A. My best recollection is that I did not. But it was

twelve years ago, so I find it impossible to be absolutely certain.

The impact of forty-seven "No"s was not lost on the jury.

Q. Did you ever take any documents from desks or wastebaskets other than your own?
A. No.
Q. Did you take these four memos in Hiss's handwriting?
A. No.
Q. The fourth handwritten note was dated March 11, 1938. Where were you on that date?
A. Sailing for Turkey from New York City.
Q. Did you ever pass any typewritten documents?
A. No.

Wadleigh examined Exhibit 10 and said that he was "quite sure" he had not taken it. He said that Cable 33 might have come across his desk, but he had no recollection of it. He pointed out that the cables on the microfilm were sent to Sayre's office and not to his division.

Q. Were you in Hiss's or Sayre's office often?
A. No. But I occasionally went there for a conference or to get a telegram initialed.

Wadleigh admitted that sometime in 1937

Chambers had taken him to dinner with Colonel Bykov. His description of Bykov differed from Chambers's, but the other details of the dinner matched Chambers's description of the dinner with Hiss and Bykov.

Cross-Examination by the Defense

The defense believed that Wadleigh had passed the documents to Chambers, since almost all of them had come from his division. Wadleigh admitted that in two years he had given four hundred or so documents to Chambers. He insisted he wasn't a traitor and refused to use the word *steal* to describe his taking of the documents. The defense asked Wadleigh to look at twenty-one documents and say whether or not he had seen them before. Four of these documents were not stamped or initialed by either Sayre or Hiss. Wadleigh admitted that he "might have seen" reports similar to these four documents. He said it was "remotely possible" that he might have seen and passed six other documents, which were on Far Eastern matters, because carbons of these documents were kept in his office's files. He said he "might have seen" twelve others, including a memo from Sayre. That memo was stamped as being from Wadleigh's division.

Q. Out of the four hundred documents you passed over, is it fair to say that you cannot tell us about a single one?

A. Well, I have a recollection of the general subject matter but no independent memory of particular ones except for one telegram from Ambassador Bullitt when he was in Russia.

> # Wadleigh Disowns Hiss Trial Papers

Headline from
The Washington Post

Be the Jury

Could Wadleigh have taken the documents from Sayre's office without being seen?

Could Wadleigh have taken carbons of the documents out of the files in his division?

How could Wadleigh have stolen the March 11 memo if he wasn't in Washington?

Could there have been another spy in the State Department?

Friday, December 9, 1949
Witness: Hede Massing
Direct Examination by the Prosecution

Massing's testimony had been barred from the first trial. The defense objected to her being a witness this time, too, but Judge Goddard overruled the objection.

Massing's first husband was a well-known German Communist, and she was affiliated with, though not a member of, the German Communist party from 1919 to 1937. In early 1934 she and her second husband, Paul Massing, began working for the Communist underground in the United States. Her husband recruited a man named Noel Field. Massing was the only witness who confirmed Chambers's claim that Hiss was a Communist and a spy. She described meeting him at a party in 1935.

Q. Did you talk with Hiss at this party?
A. Yes. I said, "I understand you are trying to get Noel Field"—who then worked in the Western Euro-

pean Division of the State Department—"away from my [espionage] group into yours." And he said, "So you are this famous girl that is trying to get Noel away from me."

The jury listened intently to Massing's every word. So did Alger Hiss. Mrs. Hiss looked at the jury most of the time as if trying to figure out what they were thinking. Massing continued:

And I said, "Yes." And he said, "Well, we will see who is going to win." Then I said, "Well, you realize you are competing with a woman." Then either he or I said something like, "Whoever is going to win, we are working for the same boss."

Q. Did you see Hiss after this party?
A. No.

Cross-Examination by the Defense

Q. Three months ago, at a party at the home of writer Eugene Lyons, did you meet Henrikas Rabinavicius?

A. I never heard of that name.

Q. At this party did you tell people about your talk with Hiss and then say to Lyons, "What happened next?" And then Lyons said, "You ought to know better than I. I wasn't there."

A. I don't remember that exactly. I probably talked a little about my relationship with Hiss. But if I said that to Lyons, it was certainly a joke.

Q. Didn't you also say that Lyons had written a book for you and you were waiting for this trial to bring it out?

A. I could not have said that because it is not so. Though I might write a book about this trial and I have talked with Lyons about his writing the articles.

Monday, December 12, 1949

Redirect by the Prosecution

After the weekend, Massing changed part of her testimony.

Q. Do you recall meeting anyone at Lyons's party?

A. I am very glad you brought this up. I thought about it over the weekend, and I remember the party very well. And I remember very well a gentleman whose name I don't recall and couldn't pronounce. But I never said the things the defense implied that I said to Mr. Lyons.

Q. When you talked with Hiss, who else was there?

A. No one. Such a talk would not be held in front of anybody else.

Be the Jury

Is Massing's story true?

Why would she lie?

Are there any other people who saw Hiss and Massing at that party together?

The prosecution rested its case.

The Defense's Strategy

In trying to cast reasonable doubt on the case against Hiss, the defense will present witnesses to

- *cast doubt* on damaging testimony given by prosecution witnesses;
- show that Hiss's *character* made him unlikely to be a spy;
- show that Hiss did not have the *means* (typewriter) to copy the documents at the time they were typed;
- show that Chambers *lied* about the meetings and trips with Hiss;
- show Chambers's *motive* for this frame-up;
- prove that Chambers *did not* see Hiss after 1937.

In addition the defense will offer other theories and evidence to explain how the documents *might have* been stolen.

The Prosecution's Strategy

The prosecutor will cross-examine the defense's witnesses and try to cast doubt on their believability and their accounts of events.

Defense Witnesses

Monday, December 12, 1949
Witness: Francis B. Sayre
Direct Examination by the Defense

Sayre had been Hiss's boss from 1936 to 1939. The defense wanted to show how much Sayre had trusted and relied on Hiss.

Q. Please describe your relationship with Hiss.

A. He was my right-hand man. I saw him intimately for two and a half years, day in and day out. He came and went into my office every day. We ate lunch together frequently. He familiarized me with the contents of hundreds of cables. Sometimes we got copies of cables about military and political things that we used for background. He often read my letters and approved them for signing.

Q. What was his attitude toward trade agreements with Russia?

A. I never saw him trying to influence American policy one way or the other. His evaluations were always based on what was best for the United States.

The defense hoped to show that Hiss wrote memos to summarize incoming mail, not to summarize for stealing.

Q. When Hiss reported to you, did he use memos?

A. Yes. Sometimes a twenty-page dispatch would come in. People would read it and clip short notes like "Agree" or "That does not hold water" on the dispatch.

Sayre produced his personal diary. It showed that on January 14, 1938, he was not in the office. On January 14, three of the stolen cables were received.

Cross-Examination by the Prosecution

The prosecutor showed Sayre the four handwritten documents. He hoped to prove that these long memos were different from Hiss's usual memos, suggesting that Hiss intentionally summarized them to steal them.

Q. Do you remember seeing these memos?

A. I cannot testify that I saw them or that I did not see them. I have no specific knowledge.

Q. Are they different from Mr. Hiss's usual memos?

A. Yes, they are quite different. Most of his memos were a few phrases. These four memos are summaries.

Q. Do you know why these four memos are neatly creased down the middle?

A. I can offer no knowledge.

Be the Jury

Why were Hiss's memos so detailed?

Why were the memos neatly folded instead of crumpled up?

Wednesday, December 14, 1949
Witness: Harry C. Hawkins
Direct Examination by the Defense

Hawkins was the head of the Trade Agreements Division, where Wadleigh worked. Hawkins examined Exhibit 50, a memo drawn up by his assistant Charles Darlington and sent to Sayre. This memo, in carbon, was photographed on microfilm. The defense set out to show that there were many carbons around for Wadleigh to steal and that he had ample opportunity to do so.

Q. Did you usually send carbons of memos to other departments?

A. No. We sent originals. But we made many carbons, which we kept in my outer file. Mr. Darlington got a carbon; my secretary got a carbon. The carbons were kept indefinitely. On important cases, we often sent an advance carbon to the division so they could start thinking about it before they got the original.

Q. Were your files and Mr. Darlington's files available to anyone in the division?

A. Yes.

Q. What was Mr. Hiss's reputation for truthfulness, loyalty, and integrity?

A. Very good.

Cross-Examination by the Prosecution

The prosecution showed that extra carbons often accompanied memos to other departments.

Q. You said when memos were sent to other divisions, carbons did not go with the original. But there was no rule against secretaries attaching carbons?

A. I do not know of any rule against it.

Q. Do you know whether or not a carbon was attached to this memo?

A. No, sir.

Q. Did you see what your secretary sent to other divisions after you signed the memo?

A. No.

The prosecutor focused on two cables that did not go to the Trade Agreements Division, where Wadleigh worked.

Q. Have you ever seen these cables before?

A. I have no real way of knowing, but based on the subject matter, I don't think they came to us.

Q. If I told you that the Records Branch said that there was no check-off for you, would you presume you did not see it?

A. Yes.

Witness: **Charles Darlington**
Direct Examination by the Defense

Darlington was Hawkins's assistant. He read over almost every paper that came in and out of the division. He identified Exhibit 50 as a memo he had prepared. His initials were on it. The defense continued to try to show how easy it was for someone to steal documents from this division.

Q. What did you send Mr. Hawkins?

A. The original, and I kept the carbon.

Q. Where did you keep the carbon?

A. It's hard to remember such details after so many years, but I believe it would have been normal for me to keep it on my desk or in one of my drawers for about two weeks, so it would be handy if Mr. Hawkins wanted to discuss it. Then I would have given it to my secretary, and she would have put it in my current file.

Q. Were your files locked?

A. No, very few files were locked. I think Mr. Hawkins had one locked file, but the rest of us didn't. I didn't lock my desk, either.

The questions shifted to Wadleigh, whom Darlington had worked with for two years.

Q. Would Mr. Wadleigh know about this memo?

A. Yes, certainly.

Q. Did Mr. Wadleigh ever ask you questions?

A. Very frequently. He was a peculiar and odd individual.

The prosecutor objected to the characterization of Wadleigh, but he was overruled. Darlington continued:

Mr. Wadleigh would frequently come in and ask questions about the work at hand. There were times he had a well-developed curiosity about a lot of things. There were times I came into my office after lunch and he would be there reading a paper on my desk. I never gave it much thought. After all, we were all part of the same group. We had confidence in each other. And he always had a good explanation for what he was doing.

Q. Did you ever see him in Mr. Sayre's office?

A. I must have seen him there fairly frequently. People in our department often talked with Mr. Hiss and Mr. Sayre.

Cross-Examination by the Prosecution

The prosecutor emphasized that there was no proof that Wadleigh had taken the stolen documents.

Q. Did you ever see Mr. Wadleigh take any papers in the department?
A. Heavens, no.
Q. Did you ever hear that he had?
A. Certainly not.
Q. Did you ever sit at other desks in your division and look at papers on a man's desk?
A. No. I think that is lacking in courtesy.
Q. How many carbons did your secretary make?
A. Probably five or six. We usually sent the carbons to other interested divisions so they could study the matter at the same time. I'm sure we did this with Exhibit Number 10. I always did that.

Be the Jury

Since almost all the stolen documents were from the Trade Agreements Division, is it possible that Wadleigh stole them?

Witness: **Geoffrey May**
Direct Examination by the Defense

The house on 30th Street

May and his wife lived in an attached house on 30th Street, next door to the Hisses. One of their windows overlooked the entrance to the Hiss house. May often saw their visitors. The defense showed May a photograph of Chambers taken around 1936. May said he had never seen anyone resembling him visit the Hisses.

Q. What color was the outside of the 30th Street house in 1936?
A. Bright yellow with vivid blue blinds. In 1938 the new tenants painted it gray with dark, gray-green blinds.

May's description of the outside colors of the Hisses' house contradicted Mrs. Chambers's.

Q. Describe the walls in your house.

A. Very thin.

Q. Did you ever hear a typewriter being used when the Hisses lived there?

A. No. But I heard one when the next tenant, a newspaper reporter, lived there. He used a typewriter a great deal.

Cross-Examination by the Prosecution

Q. You said the walls were very thin. Could you hear your neighbors' voices?

A. Yes, and they could hear ours, unless we spoke very low.

Q. When did you hear the reporter typing?

A. At home at night or during the weekends.

May visited the Hisses at Volta Place. He described that house differently from Mrs. Chambers.

Be the Jury

If Mrs. Hiss typed at night, wouldn't May have heard it?

Did anyone see Chambers visit Hiss?

What color did Mrs. Chambers say the house was?

Thursday, December 15, 1949
Witness: Claudia Catlett
Direct Examination by the Defense

Catlett was the Hisses' housekeeper from August 1935 until October 1938. She worked at their 30th Street apartment from 8 A.M. to 8 P.M. every day except Thursday afternoon and Sunday.

Q. Could you see visitors coming?

A. Yes. I looked right out the kitchen window and saw everyone coming up the front steps.

The defense showed that Chambers had been present when the FBI questioned witnesses.

Q. Tell us about your FBI interview.

A. They showed me Mr. Chambers's picture. He had a mustache then. He looked so different from most of the people who visited the Hisses. I said I had seen him once. The Hisses were both home. Mrs. Hiss asked me to fix some tea. I did. He stayed but not for long.

The FBI also showed me pictures of typewriters and asked if any of them was like Mrs. Hiss's typewriter. I said I didn't know nothing about typewriters. Then Mr. Chambers came in. He asked me about furniture and a red rug. I said I had never seen a red rug on the floor. But there was a red rug rolled up in the playroom on the fourth floor. That rug is now on the floor of the Hisses' present house.

Then he said he had slept at 30th Street overnight. I told him he didn't because they only had two bedrooms. The front bedroom, where [Hiss's stepson] Timmy slept, was just big enough for a single bed and a table. The Hisses slept in the back bedroom in a double bed. I never made up any other beds, and I took care of everything like that.

The prosecutor chose not to cross-examine Catlett.

Be the Jury

Why didn't Catlett see Chambers if he visited frequently?

Witness: **Raymond Catlett**
Direct Examination by the Defense

Raymond, Claudia Catlett's son, was twenty-seven years old. As a teenager he had done odd jobs for the Hisses.

The defense needed to prove that Hiss did not have the Woodstock typewriter during the months the documents were stolen. Catlett was shown the typewriter.

Q. When did you get this typewriter?

A. When I was about thirteen or fourteen. The Hisses gave it to me when they were moving. I think it was in December 1937. But I'm not positive.

Q. Was it in good shape?

A. No. It was broken. The end of the carriage and the roller on the right side didn't work. When you typed, the keys would kind of get stuck. And you had to push the ribbon when you typed on it and return it yourself to get ink on the keys. I played with it for a while. Then we put it in the den. We got tired of it and put it in a closet. It was there for a long time. I don't know how many months or years. My brother took it to a repair shop, but the fellow told him it couldn't be fixed. Then he gave it to my sister, Burnetta. Next Vernon Marlowe took it and kept it awhile. I finally tracked it down at Ira Lockey's.

Catlett explained that many people had access to his house and could have taken the typewriter.

Q. Were there any boarders or visitors in your house?

A. We always had boarders. In 1938 we had three. And they had lots of visitors. On weekends we had dances and parties for kids our age. Sometimes it was so crowded you couldn't move.

Q. Why did you go looking for the typewriter?

A. I told Mr. Hiss's brother, Donald, that the FBI had come about the typewriter. I thought I knew where it was. He offered to pay me $40 for the time it took me to find it.

Q. Tell us about your interview with the FBI.

A. They asked me if I knew the Hisses. They showed me some photographs of a man and lady with a baby. I said I'd never seen them. They came back to see me about ten or twelve times. Once they picked me up and took me riding in a car. They gave me beer.

Cross-Examination by the Prosecution

Catlett admitted that he could not pinpoint exactly when he had gotten the typewriter, suggesting that it might have still been with the Hisses when the documents were typed.

Q. Who in your family used the typewriter?
A. We all did. We sort of poked on it. But nobody in the house really did too much with it until Burnetta went to college and used it.
Q. When the FBI asked you about the Hiss typewriter, did you tell them about the Woodstock?
A. No, sir.
Q. But you did tell Donald Hiss?
A. Yes, I did.
Q. Did he suggest giving you money to find it?
A. No, but the next time I saw him I said I might need some money, and he offered $40.

The prosecution challenged Catlett's story about the FBI so the jury would not think the FBI had done anything improper.

Q. Tell us about this beer party with the FBI.
A. Well, we left the FBI office after 9 P.M. They picked up some beer and we drove around. One man was asking me questions. One agent kept punching another guy. I drank the beer down real quick, and they said, "Here, have another." And I drank another

and another. I think I drank most of the beer. Then they dropped me off at home.

Q. Is this the first time you told anyone about the beer?

A. Yes, sir. No one at the last trial asked me about this or the $200 the FBI man offered me to find the typewriter.

Catlett identified FBI agent Courtland Jones, who was in the courtroom, as the man who offered him the $200.

Be the Jury

When did the Catletts get the typewriter?

If the typewriter was in such poor condition, how could Burnetta have used it for school?

Could someone have stolen the typewriter out of the Catletts' house?

Why did the FBI give Catlett beer?

Witness: **Joseph R. Boucot**

Boucot owned the cottage in Smithtown that Chambers and his wife rented in July and August 1935 when they were using the alias Breen. Boucot's cottage was a hundred feet away from their cottage. Boucot testified that he saw "Mrs. Breen" quite a few times and was in their cottage several times for coffee. He said he never saw Mrs. Hiss there.

Witness: **Norma Brown**

Boucot's sister had spent two weeks in August 1935 with her brother. She testified that she had met the "Breens" but had never seen or met anyone else staying with them.

The defense believed Boucot's and Brown's testimony demolished Mrs. Chambers's story that Mrs. Hiss visited her that summer.

Be the Jury

Did Mrs. Hiss visit Smithtown?

Friday, December 16, 1949
Witness: Lucy Davis

The defense needed to prove that the Peterborough trip on August 9 and 10, 1937, never took place. Lucy Davis ran Bleakhouse, the fourteen-room guest house in Peterborough where Chambers said he and the Hisses had stayed overnight. Bleakhouse was opened August 1,

1937. Davis testified that she was on the premises twenty-four hours a day. Davis said that she had never seen the Hisses or Chambers before the trial. She produced the guest book. All guests registered when they arrived. The guest book was kept on a desk directly opposite the front door. She remembered all three guests who had visited before August 13.

Be the Jury

If all guests had to sign the register, why weren't the names of Chambers and Hiss in it?

Witness: Harry C. Coleman
Direct Examination by the Defense

Coleman was a teller in the Kent County Savings Bank in Chestertown, Maryland. The Hisses said they spent July 15 to August 15, 1937, in an apartment two blocks from the bank and never left the town during that time. A copy of Hiss's checking-account statement was submitted in evidence. It showed a deposit of $100 on August 9, 1937. The defense believed this established that Hiss was in Chestertown, not Peterborough, on August 9.

Q. Does this August 9th deposit mean that the bank received that check on August 9th?
A. Yes.
Q. When did the bank open on August 9, 1937?
A. At 9 A.M.
Q. How far is it from Chestertown to Washington?
A. About a hundred miles.

Cross-Examination by the Prosecution

Q. The deposit date says August 9. But do you have any way of telling whether that deposit was made at the bank in person or whether you received it in the morning's mail?

A. No, sir.

Be the Jury

Did Hiss deposit the check or mail it?

Witness: **Thomas Fansler**
Direct Examination by the Defense

Fansler was Priscilla Hiss's brother. He explained that he visited the Hisses in Chestertown from Friday, August 6, until late Monday morning, August 9, when they drove him to Wilmington, Delaware, to get a train to New York. He didn't remember the exact time the train left but he said it was considerably after breakfast.

His other testimony disputed Mrs. Chambers's claim that in 1936 the two couples had spent New Year's Eve together.

Q. What did you do Christmas 1936?
A. We spent Christmas Eve and part of Christmas Day with Alger and Priscilla and Timmy at our Manhattan apartment. On the afternoon of Christmas Day both families drove to Chappaqua, New York, to see friends. My family went back to New York on December 27. The Hisses stayed on. Priscilla stayed later than Alger because Timmy had chicken pox.
Q. Do you personally know where Mrs. Hiss was on New Year's Eve?
A. No.

Cross-Examination by the Prosecution

Q. How long is it from Chestertown to Wilmington?

A. It's about forty-five to fifty miles, I guess. A little over an hour by car.

Q. When did you leave on Monday?

A. I don't exactly remember, except that it was sometime late morning.

Be the Jury

Might Fansler lie to save his sister's husband?

3 Hiss Witnesses Dispute Chambers

Headline from *The Washington Post*

Witness: **Tennis Collier**
Direct Examination by the Defense

Collier, a builder, had remodeled houses on 30th Street and done work at Volta Place.

Q. Tell us what you did at Volta Place.

A. Well, this sketch shows the house before 1946. The photograph shows the house after the remodeling. We built an addition for a maid's room. You can see the windows we put in. We put a concrete slab on top of the maid's room, covered it with flagstone, and built an iron railing around it.

maid's room

Volta Place before 1946   after remodeling

Q. What color was the brick before you added all this?

A. Reddish—brick color.

Q. What was the color of the living room at the 30th Street house?

A. Green.

Cross-Examination by the Prosecution

The prosecution believed it was unrealistic that Collier could remember the colors of these houses so many years later.

Q. What is the present color of the 30th Street house?

A. It has been yellow since 1947.

Q. What was the color of the brick wall at Volta Place in 1938?

A. Red—like bricks.

Q. What makes you so sure?

A. I've worked on that house so many times. And I have worked in that area for thirty-one years.

Q. Are you telling us you can remember the different colors of thousands of those houses?

A. No. But I can remember a house we have been in so many times and worked on. I am just as confident that the wall was red as anything I know.

Be the Jury

What color did Mrs. Chambers say Volta Place was?

What color did she say the 30th Street living room was?

Monday, December 19, 1949
Witness: Malcolm Cowley
Direct Examination by the Defense

Cowley was a writer. The defense believed his testimony showed that Chambers constantly lied.

Q. Tell us about seeing Chambers on December 13, 1940.

A. We met in a restaurant. He was wearing gray clothes and a dirty shirt. Both looked like they had been slept in. His teeth were in very bad condition. One or more was missing. He was writing an article for *Time* magazine about writers who had been sympathetic to communism. We talked briefly about the article. He mentioned Communists he knew in the federal government. I had never heard of any of them. Then he mentioned Francis B. Sayre. I said, "Sayre, President Wilson's son-in-law?" And he said, "Yes." Then I said, "But he's the high commissioner to the Philippines." He said, "Yes, that's him. He was the head of a Communist underground group in the State Department." He never mentioned Hiss.

Cowley showed his diary. It contained notes he had written right after that meeting.

Cross-Examination by the Prosecution

The prosecution insinuated that Cowley might have heard incorrectly.

Q. Were you always hard of hearing?
A. Not at that time. My hearing was quite effective, especially listening over a lunch table. My hearing still is fine for distances under twelve feet.

The prosecution tried to discredit Cowley by revealing that he had once been sympathetic to communism.

Q. Did you associate with Communists?
A. Yes. From 1932 to 1939.
Q. Were you once sympathetic to communism?
A. Yes.

Be the Jury

Why did Chambers accuse Sayre of being a Communist?

Monday, December 26, and Tuesday, December 27, 1949
Witness: Alger Hiss
Direct Examination by the Defense

The Fifth Amendment to the United States Constitution says that in a criminal case, defendants do not have to testify against themselves. Hiss willingly testified, believing his testimony would convince the jury that Chambers had lied.

When Hiss walked to the witness stand, the difference between his outward refinement and Chambers's untidy appearance and coarse looks was evident. Hiss was handsome, slim, and elegantly dressed. He spoke softly and answered in a formal, precise manner, often asking for a question to be clarified before he answered it.

The defense asked him to recount his impressive government career. Then Hiss contradicted all of Chambers's testimony, starting with the "rental" of his 28th Street apartment.

Q. When did you first meet Whittaker Chambers?
A. Sometime in late December 1934 or early January 1935, he came to my office. I was working for the Senate Nye Committee. He said he was writing articles on our munitions investigation. He asked me questions. I suggested he look at some of our written material. About two weeks later, he came back and read through these documents. They were all public information. A couple of weeks later he telephoned and asked to meet again. We met for lunch. I often did that when people wanted to talk to me. Three weeks later, he told me he was planning to come to Washington with his family but didn't have a place to stay. I was moving and had an old apartment on my hands for two or three months. I hadn't intended to sublease it. In fact I had already told the electric company to disconnect the lights as of May 1, 1935. But when he mentioned it, I suggested he take the apartment and pay me $60 a month to cover my costs. He agreed. The day he was supposed to move in, he telephoned me up and told me that his furnishings were delayed. I offered to put him up until his furniture arrived. It turned out he stayed three nights because the van didn't arrive.

Hiss denied Chambers's story of the trip to Peterborough. He testified that he had been in Chestertown, Maryland, from the middle of

July through the middle of August. He had deposited the $100 check in person at the bank on August 9. Then he explained why he had given his old car to Chambers.

Q. Did you see Mr. Crosley during the fall of 1935?
A. Yes. I don't remember why we got together, but I do remember telling him that I had bought a new car, and that he could have my old Ford as I had promised him. I gave him the certificate of title for the car. A couple of months later he brought the car back and said he didn't have any use for it then and wondered if I would take care of it. So that winter I kept it for him on the streets. He picked up the car sometime in the spring of 1936, and I never saw it again.

Hiss examined the certificate of title. He insisted that when he received it the reassignment of title was blank and William Rosen's name wasn't there. Hiss had filled in the name of Cherner Motor Company; Cherner was the company taking care of the transfer. Hiss explained that a lawyer friend notarized his signature, as required by law. The lawyer was no longer living. The sales records at Cherner, which would have shown the details of the transfer to Rosen, were missing.

Q. Did you ever know that Mr. Chambers was a Communist or in the Communist underground?
A. No.
Q. Are you or have you ever been a Communist or been in sympathy with Communist ideas?
A. No, sir.

Hiss explained how he had gotten the Oriental rug from Chambers.

Q. When else did you see Mr. Crosley?
A. Sometime in spring 1936. I am not sure of the date. He came to my house. He gave me a red Oriental rug with a fringe on it. He said some wealthy patron had given it to him, and he was giving it to me. I think my wife was there, but I'm not sure.
Q. When did you see him next?
A. When he came to pick up the Ford, sometime at the end of May or early June. I don't remember if it was then or over the telephone, but he requested an-

other small loan. He had taken a few small loans—
maybe amounting to $30—from me during the time
I knew him. But he had not repaid me. I told him
then that I didn't think he was ever going to repay
me what he owed me. I thought we had better forget
about that money and not see each other anymore.

Q. Did you ever see him after that?

A. Not until the HUAC hearings. I had been shown
pictures of him before, but I didn't recognize him.
Even at the hearings I
had trouble recogniz-
ing him. When I knew
him in 1934, he was a
short, heavyset man
with very bad teeth. In
1948 his teeth had
been fixed and it had
changed the shape of
his mouth, and he had
lost considerable weight,
and that had also
changed his appear-
ance.

Snapshot of Chambers in 1934

Hiss answered all questions with a soft, calm
voice. He was more poised and less nervous
than he had been in his first trial. He explained
that he had told HUAC the same facts he was
telling in court today.

The fact that Chambers had bought a farm in Maryland that Hiss had once tried to buy was damaging evidence. The defense tried to show it was a coincidence.

Q. Did you try to buy a farm in Westminster, Maryland?
A. Yes. In November 1935, Mrs. Hiss saw an ad in a Baltimore newspaper and contacted a real estate agent. We saw the property and put a deposit on it, and I think signed a contract to buy it. About five months later, the realtor told me that the original price had gone up. I told him I was no longer interested.

Hiss showed his letters to the real estate agent.

For over three hours Hiss continued denying Chambers's accusations: He had never given him any furniture. He had not loaned him $400 to buy a car. In fact, when Hiss had gone to buy his new car, he had taken out a bank loan because he didn't have enough money. Hiss explained that his wife had withdrawn $400 from their bank account to buy furnishings for their new house on Volta Place.

As for New Year's Eve 1936, Hiss testified that he returned to Washington from Chappaqua on either December 27 or 28, but his wife stayed through New Year's Day. He showed a letter to his wife postmarked December 30, 1936. The defense believed the letter confirmed that Priscilla was not in Washington on that New Year's Eve, for why would Hiss write her if he was seeing her the next day?

Hiss also explained how things worked in his office to show that someone could have gotten in to steal the documents.

Q. Did you ever leave papers on your desk?

A. Yes. If I went out of the office during the day or when I went out to lunch, I would normally leave any papers I was working with on my desk. And I left my door open.

Q. Did people seeing Mr. Sayre ever stop in your room?

A. If they got there ahead of time or if he was behind schedule, they might drop in my room to chat. Sometimes I came into my office and found people waiting there for me or for Mr. Sayre. They had probably been told we would be coming back shortly.

Q. Did Mr. Wadleigh ever visit your offices?

A. I don't remember how many times he came or the particular dates. But he came several times to Mr. Sayre's office and came to talk to me. Maybe he was bringing a telegram to get initialed by Mr. Sayre or wanted to discuss something with me.

Q. Did you work with people from the Trade Agreements Division?

A. Yes, frequently. Mr. Darlington worked in my office a number of times.

Be the Jury

Why did Hiss lend money to somone he hardly knew?

Why would Hiss lend Chambers $400 when he didn't have enough money to buy himself a car?

Why didn't Hiss tell Chambers and his family to go to a hotel for those few days instead of letting them stay at his house?

Could someone have stolen papers from Hiss's desk?

Tuesday, December 27–Thursday, December 29, 1949

Cross-Examination by the Prosecution

The prosecution tried to show that Hiss's story about withdrawing $400 from the bank to buy furnishings didn't ring true.

Q. When you took out this $400, didn't you have a checking account and charge accounts in several stores?
A. Yes, we had charges in some of the bigger stores. But my wife wanted to buy a couple of chairs and some prints of modern paintings at shops where we did not have charge accounts. And we did charge some other furnishings.

Q. Do you have canceled checks to prove that?
A. No, in 1947, when we moved to New York, we destroyed all our checks from ten years before.

Q. Did your stepson go to Washington during the summer of 1937?
A. Definitely not.

To discredit Hiss's testimony, the prosecutor tried to make Hiss's rental agreement with Chambers seem foolish.

Q. Before you rented him the apartment, did you check out his credit or ask other reporters about him?
A. No.

Q. Did you charge him for using your furniture, and the gas, the electric, and the telephone?

A. No.

Q. When he gave you that rug later, did he say specifically, "Here is a rug worth so many dollars, which I would like you to consider as payment for that money I owe you for the rent"?

A. No, he didn't say anything specific like that.

Q. Do you consider that rug an overpayment or an underpayment?

A. I considered it an inadequate payment.

The prosecutor tried to show that Hiss's story of the transfer of the car was also unbelievable.

Q. Why did you give him your car?

A. He said he needed a car, so I told him that I would let him have my old Ford when I got a new car.

Q. So this man to whom you made an oral lease, and made no profit from, and whom you had no idea who he was other than the name he told you—you promised him a Ford when you bought a new car?

A. I said he could have it. I don't know whether I would call it an actual promise.

Q. As a lawyer didn't you realize that if Mr. Chambers had an accident with your car, you might be sued?

A. I never thought about the possibility.

Q. And after he used this car for a while and then told you he couldn't keep it anymore, you just agreed to be responsible for taking care of it during the winter?

A. Yes.

The prosecutor tried to show that Hiss had associated with other Communists.

Q. Did you ever know people who were Communists?

A. I have never known anybody whom I knew to be a Communist. I knew some people at law school and in the government who it was said were Communists.

Hiss was asked about many specific men, all of whom had been accused by Chambers of being Communists. Hiss said that he knew them all.

The prosecutor showed check stubs for the storage of the Oriental rug for nine months, including three months after the Hisses had moved into Volta Place. The prosecution believed the rug was stored because it incriminated Hiss.

Be the Jury

Why was Hiss so kind to Chambers when he hardly knew him?

Why did Hiss agree to take back the car that winter when it must have been inconvenient?

Did Hiss put the rug in storage to hide it?

Who is telling the truth: Hiss or Chambers?

Friday, December 30, 1949–Thursday, January 5, 1950
Witness: Priscilla Hiss
Direct Examination by the Defense

Though witnesses usually aren't allowed to be in the courtroom before they testify, Priscilla Hiss was there throughout the trial. This was not a special privilege. The prosecution believed that she had typed the documents. No formal charges had been made against her, but as an unindicted co-conspirator she had the right to hear evidence against her.

When Mrs. Hiss took the witness stand, she removed the white gloves that had covered her hands throughout the trial. She denied all of Chambers's accusations, reinforcing her husband's version of events. She said she had given the typewriter away because the keys sometimes stuck and the ribbon puckered. She wanted her son to learn to type on a new typewriter.

Q. Did you type these documents?

A. No.

Q. Are you a touch typist?

A. No.

Q. How long would it have taken you to type a single-spaced sixteen-page document?

A. I don't know.

Mrs. Hiss Denies Typing Documents

Headline from *The Washington Post*

She spoke almost as softly as Esther Chambers had and was repeatedly asked to speak louder.

Q. Have you ever been a Communist?

A. No.

Q. Did you ever attend any Socialist meetings?

A. No. When we lived in New York City, I gave money to a soup kitchen run by the Socialist party. I worked there making sandwiches and serving food, but I wasn't a member of the Socialist party.

Cross-Examination by the Prosecution

Q. Were you sufficiently familiar with a typewriter to have typed the documents?

A. I think so.

Q. You said you weren't a member of the Socialist party. How do you explain that your name is on the 1932 records of the Morningside Branch of the Socialist party as being a member of the Socialist party?

A. I don't know.

Be the Jury

If she isn't a touch typist, could she have typed a sixteen-page document in one night?

If she isn't a member of the Socialist party, why is her name in their records?

Monday, January 9–
Wednesday, January 11, 1950
Witness: Dr. Carl Binger
Direct Examination by the Defense

Binger, a psychiatrist, had sat through the first trial, expecting to testify about Chambers's mental condition, but his testimony had not been allowed. When Binger's name was called this time, the prosecutor objected again, but this time the judge let him testify. Binger's opinion was based on Chambers's testimony and behavior on the witness stand at both trials and on his writings.

The defense asked Binger a forty-five-minute-long question that covered many damaging facts about Chambers. Part of the question was:

Q. Now Doctor, assume that the following facts are true: that Chambers got into trouble in high school over a speech; that he had trouble with college authorities over a play; that in 1925 he joined the Communist party; that he used many false names; that he changed his testimony many times; that he did not believe in God; that when he visited Hiss he was poorly dressed; that he had a brother who committed suicide; that he hid microfilm in a pumpkin; that he accused Hiss of espionage and testified that Hiss was perhaps his closest friend. . . .

If these facts are true, what is your opinion of his mental condition?

A. I think he has a mental disease known as a psychopathic personality. Psychopaths are deceptive and often paranoid. They have abnormal sexuality and abnormal emotionality. They may be alcoholics or drug addicts. Their actions are often bizarre. They are untidy. They cannot form stable attachments. They constantly lie. They often withhold information and often steal.

The psychopath knows what he is doing but he does not always know why he does it. His acts are frequently impulsive and often bizarre, so they don't make much sense to ordinary people. Psychopaths believe that their fantasies are true. They may be a hero at one moment and a gangster at the next. They claim friendships where none exist, just as they make accusations which have no basis in fact. Chambers has all the marks of a classic psychopath except alcoholism and drug addiction.

Binger gave examples: Chambers had stolen books from the Columbia Library and documents from the federal government. His untidiness was seen in his disheveled appearance and his bad teeth, which he only recently had had fixed. He had withheld information from the

FBI and HUAC. His pathological lying was seen in his using aliases and his accusations against Hiss.

Chambers Is Called 'Pathological Liar'

Headline from
The Washington Post

Binger pointed out that Chambers had often stared at the ceiling during his testimony, as if he were trying to remember what he had said before. Binger said planting the microfilm in the pumpkin was bizarre behavior; thinking he would be murdered for defecting from communism was paranoid thinking. Binger labeled Chambers's emotional paralysis after his brother died as abnormal emotionality.

Cross-Examination by the Prosecution

> # Hiss Psychiatrist Quizzed for Hours

Headline from
The Washington Post

For three days the prosecution questioned Binger, trying to show that his diagnosis was based on very little knowledge.

Q. Aren't you making this diagnosis without much information on his early childhood and adolescence?

A. My diagnosis is based on thirty years of his behavior.

Q. Would a psychopath hold a ten-year job at *Time*?

A. Working around the clock as Chambers did usually means an emotional disturbance.

Q. Isn't being married for nineteen years and being the father of two children evidence of stable attachments?

A. It depends on the kind of attachment.

Q. Is there any evidence that Chambers deliberately and vengefully hurt a friend?

A. I don't recall his mentioning any friends except Hiss.

Q. You said hiding the microfilm in the pumpkin was bizarre. What about the colonists hiding the Connecticut Charter from the British in an oak tree?

A. That was not bizarre because that took place over two hundred years ago in a very primitive community. Hiding microfilm in a pumpkin is not how a modern person behaves.

The prosecution ridiculed Binger's analysis and his behavior in court.

Q. Albert Einstein and Thomas Edison didn't dress very well either. Was this pathological?
A. One must look at the whole picture of a person's personality.
Q. I noticed you glanced at the ceiling fifty-nine times in fifty minutes. Is this a symptom of a psychopathic personality?
A. Not alone.

The prosecutor believed there were reasonable explanations for many of Chambers's actions.

Q. When Chambers lied when he was a Communist, wasn't he acting like a soldier for a cause he believed in?
A. I see it as another lie in a series of lies.

Be the Jury

Is Chambers mentally disturbed?

Is it likely he is lying about Hiss?

Witness: **Henrikas Rabinavicius**

Rabinavicius, a former Lithuanian diplomat, testified that Hede Massing had lied on the stand. He explained that Hiss and Noel Field were not at the State Department at the same time, so Hiss could not have tried to recruit him then. He described his conversation with Mrs. Massing at Eugene Lyons's party:

I said, "During your conversation with Hiss, did he tell you he was a Communist or a spy?" She said, "No. He didn't tell me. I knew he was." I asked her, "How could you know if he didn't tell you?" And she said, "You don't understand. One spy recognizes another spy."

Twenty-seven people appeared as character witnesses for Hiss. Among them were Supreme Court Justice Felix Frankfurter, who had known Hiss when he was a law student at Harvard and had recommended him to serve as law clerk for Justice Holmes. Justice Stanley Reed said that Hiss's reputation at the Justice Department was one of "integrity, loyalty, and veracity." Some others who testified to his integrity were Admiral Arthur J. Hepburn; Calvert Magruder, chief judge of the U.S. Court of Appeals for the First Circuit (Boston); and Governor Adlai Stevenson of Illinois.

Be the Jury

Who do I trust more: Chambers or Hiss?

Rebuttal Witnesses

Tuesday, January 17, 1950
Witness: Dr. Margaret Mary Nicholson
Direct Examination by the Prosecution

Nicholson's office records showed that she had seen Hiss's stepson, Timmy, at home on January 2, 3, and 6 of 1937. The prosecution believed this cast doubt that Mrs. Hiss had been in Chappaqua on New Year's Eve 1936. Her records also showed that she had seen Timmy on August 15, 1937.

Be the Jury

Do her records prove that the Hisses were in Washington New Year's Eve 1936?

Where were the Hisses on August 15?

Witness: **Burnetta Fisher**

Fisher was Raymond Catlett's sister. She identified the Woodstock typewriter as the one her
brothers gave her when she was in junior or senior high. She said the typewriter was in working condition and that she typed notes for her
classes on it. She did not remember the specific
date she received the typewriter, but thought it
was about 1938.

Witness: **Courtland Jones**

Jones was one of the FBI agents who had questioned Raymond Catlett. He denied Catlett's
story that he had tried to bribe him.

Witness: **Edith Murray**
Direct Examination by the Prosecution

Murray was a housekeeper for the Chamberses. She knew them under the alias Cantwell. Chambers had told her he was a traveling salesman. She worked from 9:30 A.M. to 6:30 P.M. six days a week.

Q. Did the Chamberses have any visitors?
A. Only two I know of. A lady, called Miss Priscilla, who said she lived in Washington. She stayed overnight when Mrs. Cantwell went to New York to see the doctor. I asked her if she had any children and she said she had one little boy. The lady also came another night with her husband when I was in the kitchen finishing up my work. I greeted them at the door.

Murray identified the two visitors as the Hisses.

The defense objected to Murray's testimony. The opposite side must be given a list of witnesses well in advance of the trial. The defense said that her last-minute appearance didn't give him enough time to check out her story. The judge overruled the objection.

Cross-Examination by the Defense

Q. How many times did you see this woman?

A. Four times. Three alone and once with her husband. But there probably were other times. She usually came about 10 A.M., and stayed until afternoon. Mrs. Cantwell was always very happy to see her.

The defense believed Murray had been coached by the FBI to identify the Hisses.

Q. When the FBI showed you Mrs. Hiss's photo, what did you say?

A. I said it looked like someone I knew, maybe a movie actress. I knew I had seen her but I didn't know where. Later the FBI told me I was going to a place to see if I could recognize the people in the photographs. We went to the hall outside this courtroom. After a while I saw Mr. and Mrs. Hiss.

Q. Did you ever read about the case in the newspaper?

A. No, sir. In 1942 I had a nervous breakdown. The doctor told me not to read anything that would upset me. So I don't know anything about the case.

Be the Jury

Is Murray the only witness to have seen Mrs. Chambers and the Hisses together?

The Defense's Closing Statement

Thursday, January 19, 1950

Now that both sides had presented their witnesses, the lawyers made closing statements. They summarized their viewpoints, contradicted and discredited the evidence from the other side, and appealed to the jury's emotions. Listen carefully to the defense's closing statement. Separate the facts from his emotional presentation, for your verdict must be based on facts, not emotions.

There are two charges of perjury against Alger Hiss. The first charge says that he lied when he said that he did not pass Chambers secret documents in February or March 1938. The second charge says he lied when he said he did not see Chambers after January 1,

1937. To convict Hiss, you must believe Chambers and find corroborating evidence, for Chambers is the only person to testify that Hiss passed him secret documents. And remember how many times Chambers lied.

Remember at this trial when Chambers told the prosecutor that all these documents were given to him by Alger Hiss? But later when I asked him, "Are you sure you got Exhibit 10 from Hiss?" He answered, "I am not that sure. It was the kind of stuff that Harry Dexter White gave me." I don't understand that answer. Chambers spent months reviewing the stolen documents with the FBI. Before this trial he swore four times under oath that he got all of them from Hiss. And yet here, for the first time, he says that he thinks he got Exhibit 10 from White, a dead man who can't answer these charges.

Now what is important about Exhibit 10? It was not typed on the Woodstock. The only office in the State Department that received Exhibit 10 was the Far Eastern Division. Was there a spy in that division? We know that there was a spy in the Trade Agreements Division. The spy was Julian Wadleigh.

And what about this supposed visit by Chambers and Hiss to meet Bykov? Remember how differently Wadleigh described Bykov from Chambers. And why didn't Bykov testify and confirm Chambers's testimony?

Mr. and Mrs. Chambers told about certain meetings with the Hisses, but they never testified about the same meetings. Mr. Chambers said that around Christmas of 1937 the Hisses visited their Mount Royal Terrace house. But at other times he testified about a New Year's Eve party. Before the trial Mrs. Chambers said she did not remember ever seeing the Hisses at Mount Royal Terrace. But at this trial she said the Hisses celebrated their wedding anniversary there in December 1937. She said she saw the Hisses at Auchentoroly Terrace, but Mr. Chambers had no recollection of this. Mrs. Chambers said the two couples were together on New Year's Eve 1936. But we have a letter that Hiss wrote to his wife in Chappaqua, New York, on December 29, 1936. She could not have received this letter before New Year's Eve. In it Mr. Hiss says how sorry he is that Timmy had exposed the other children to chicken pox. Mr. Hiss told his wife to stay in Chappaqua over the weekend. Mrs. Hiss did not return to Washington for New Year's Eve.

Chambers used aliases all the time. He told us that it was quite possible that he used the name Crosley.

After seeing Hiss a couple of times in his office and at lunch, Chambers said he needed a car and an apartment. Hiss generously offered his old apartment for two months at $60 per month including his old car. It was not a bad deal for Hiss. If Chambers had really paid him, it would have been a good deal. The Hisses had already notified the electric company to disconnect the electricity in their old apartment before he offered the apartment to Chambers.

Now about that old Ford. Chambers used the Ford in the fall of 1935 and took possession of it in spring 1936. If Hiss was a Communist, would he have told HUAC that Chambers had borrowed his car a number of times and then that he had turned it over to Chambers?

Cherner Motor Car Company sent the title papers to Hiss to sign. Hiss wrote in the name of Cherner Motor Company, indicating that he insisted on knowing who the transferee was to be before he signed it. Mr. Smith, a lawyer who worked down the hall from Hiss, notarized this signing. If there had been anything sinister, do you suppose Hiss would have let a government official do this? Hiss left blank the reassignment of the title of the car, because he didn't know it was going to anybody else but Chambers. Only Chambers knew that. Remember on the Ford, as with everything else, you only have the testimony of an admitted perjurer, an admitted liar.

Chambers says he gave Hiss an Oriental rug in December 1936 in appreciation from the Russian people for what Hiss had done. But Chambers testified that Hiss met Bykov in January 1937. Now why did he give Hiss the rug before Hiss had supposedly seen

Bykov? The truth is that Hiss took the rug in place of the money that Chambers owed him. He still has it on his floor. Is that the action of a man who is hiding something?

Mr. and Mrs. Chambers testified that Mrs. Hiss visited them in a cottage in Smithtown. They said that Mrs. Hiss met the landlord and his sister. But these people, living at a cottage one hundred feet away, testified that they never saw her.

If there is anything in this case that has been definitely proven to have never taken place, it is this weird story about the Peterborough trip. Hiss could not have been in Peterborough on August 9 because he was in Chestertown, Maryland, that day. How do we know? Because we have his bank deposit made that day to the Chestertown bank. The bank opens at 9 A.M. The bank is two blocks away from where the Hisses were staying. Hiss walked there and deposited the check. We also have Thomas Fansler's testimony that he was with the Hisses in Chestertown on Monday, August 9. And Mrs. Davis never saw the Hisses or Chamberses at Bleakhouse. The Peterborough trip never took place.

Chambers said Hiss loaned him $400 to buy a new car. On November 19, 1937, Mrs. Hiss withdrew $400 from the bank to buy things for the new apartment. She didn't make a record of it because there was no need to. Around that time Hiss also bought a new car. And how did he pay for it? He turned in his old car, got $325 in the trade-in, and paid off the rest in twelve monthly payments. If Hiss didn't have enough money to buy his car outright, why would he loan money to Chambers?

So how did Chambers know about this $400 withdrawal? The FBI knew about this bank withdrawal on January 31, 1949. At that time Chambers was spending day after day with the FBI. Now I am not criticizing anything the FBI did. But this case shows times of overzealousness on the part of some FBI men. So I can imagine some agent saying to Chambers, "Well, I notice a withdrawal from Hiss's bank account on November 19, 1937, of $400. Did you have any transaction then?" And then Chambers says, "Oh, yes, he loaned me that money for a car." I say this because the first time Chambers ever testified about that $400 loan was after the FBI had the bank records. And why didn't Mrs. Chambers know about this supposed loan? She has said that his mother probably gave them the money for the car. His mother had given them money very often.

Chambers hired investigators to find out about the colors of the houses and the furniture. But the investigators gave them many inaccurate details. Mrs. Chambers said the outside of the 30th Street house was white, but it was a garish yellow. She said that the brick walls at Volta Place were white, but they were red. She talked about a concrete porch, which wasn't put there until 1946.

And what about these weekly meetings that Chambers said took place between 5 P.M. and 6 P.M.? Claudia Catlett always answered the door. But Mrs. Catlett testified that she only saw Chambers once.

The prosecution said Mrs. Hiss typed the documents at night. But their neighbor, Geoffrey May, said he never heard a typewriter at night. And he would have heard it, because after the Hisses moved, a reporter moved in, and created much annoyance at night when he typed.

Wadleigh said the only time he ever saw Chambers was on a dark street corner when he passed him the briefcase or when he got back the briefcase. Wadleigh never met Mrs. Chambers. He was never in their home. Chambers was never at the Wadleighs'. That is how fellow conspirators treat each other. Hiss would have been crazy, if he had ever had any criminal connection with Chambers, to go to his house and go on trips with him.

When Chambers was asked to produce evidence that Hiss was a Communist, he produced an envelope with the secret documents. But no one saw him open the envelope and pull out the documents. And every document in the microfilm could have been used against Francis Sayre as well as against Alger Hiss. And it is clear from what Mr. Cowley told us that at one time Chambers planned to falsely accuse Mr. Sayre.

Chambers said all the documents on the microfilm were photographed at one time and that they all came from one person. But Exhibit 10 did not go to Sayre's or Hiss's office, so how could Hiss be the thief who stole these documents?

The stolen documents were typed on the Woodstock. The last document is dated April 1, 1938. Who typed it? How did Chambers get them typed on the Woodstock? Anybody who can get top-secret documents out of the State Department would not have much trouble locating this big typewriter. Maybe Chambers had someone visit the Catletts and say they had come to repair the Woodstock. He wouldn't have had much difficulty locating Catlett's house. The door was always open. There were always people coming and going.

As to the question of Hiss's motive to be a spy: The government has failed entirely to suggest a motive unless it be this vague suggestion that he was a Communist. Mr. Rabinavicius testified that Mrs. Massing said that Hiss and Field were in the same department. But Hiss didn't go there until after Field left, so how could Hiss recruit him as a spy when they never saw each other? Mrs. Massing's testimony is not true.

Why didn't Chambers tell the truth right away? Why did he lie so many times? Why did he lie here? Dr. Binger testified that Chambers is a psychopath. That's why he lied so many times. A psychopath is easily influenced to turn against someone and use methods such as have been described here. When Hiss told Chambers he was a deadbeat, Chambers didn't forget.

In coming to a close, let me contrast the two men. Hiss lived a normal life of an American boy. Chambers was brought up in a home that was skeptically indifferent to religion. When Hiss graduated from college, he went to law school. Chambers dropped out of college and became a fanatical Communist. His brother had asked him to join into a suicide pact. In 1932, when Hiss was in New York working as a lawyer, Chambers was in the Communist underground. In 1936 and 1937, when Chambers was getting secret documents from Wadleigh, Hiss was working at the State Department. Everyone who knew Hiss highly respected him.

I believe in the innocence and honesty of my client, and I believe by your verdict you will put the stamp of honesty on Alger Hiss.

The Prosecution's Closing Statement

Friday, January 20, 1950

Now listen to the prosecution's closing statement. Remember to separate the facts from the emotional presentation, for your verdict must be based on facts, not emotions.

Alger Hiss is a well-respected lawyer with a good reputation. But remember that Benedict Arnold, a major general in the Revolutionary Army, with an equally good reputation, sold out to the enemy. And remember that the defendant lied to the grand jury and they believed Chambers.

An unprejudiced psychiatrist can tell much about a person's mind from studying the person and giving tests. But Dr. Binger did not examine Chambers. If I thought there was a serious question of Chambers's mental condition, I would have called psychiatrists.

Chambers was on the stand for six days. He was sincere. He did not evade questions.

Chambers does not deny that he became a Communist. But in 1939, when he was back loving his country, he saw the dangers of communism. So he told the authorities that Communists were in our government.

Now did these two men know each other well? Fact Number 1: Chambers said he lived in Hiss's apartment on 28th Street. Hiss admitted it. Some mooch comes and says he can't find an apartment, and you give him one, and throw in the furniture and the gas and electric and the phone, and an old Ford. Imagine a lawyer making such a deal.

Fact Number 2: Chambers said Hiss gave away his old Ford to the Communist party. Hiss said he had a Ford and Chambers used it. The car ended up with Rosen. Does that confirm what Chambers says? Yes.

Fact Number 3: The rug. Count II of the indictment says Hiss didn't see Chambers after January 1, 1937. But Professor Schapiro showed us the invoices from the rug dealer who shipped two rugs to Washington around December 29, 1936. And Mr. Hiss told you, "He gave me a rug; I have it."

Fact Number 4: Chambers got furniture from the Hisses. He has that furniture on his farm today. He told us Mr. McLean saw it.

Fact Number 5: On August 9, 1937, Chambers

went up to Peterborough to see Harry Dexter White. He parked at the end of White's driveway where the Hisses could not see. He showed you the photograph. Ladies and gentlemen, that is corroboration.

Mrs. Massing confirmed that the two men knew each other. And Mrs. Catlett said she saw Chambers at the Hisses' home.

Chambers said the Hisses gave him $400 to buy a car. What is the proof? Hiss withdrew $400 from the bank a day or two before Chambers bought the car. Now the defense didn't say Chambers saw the bankbook. No, they didn't say that. But they knew this because he did say, "Well, perhaps the FBI showed Chambers that bank account." That statement sort of makes the FBI a conspirator with Chambers. Can you imagine that? This is open season on the FBI. Everybody is taking potshots at the FBI. That's the Communist party line. If you think any evidence in this case was manufactured by the FBI, acquit Alger Hiss.

Both Mr. and Mrs. Chambers described the various Hiss houses. How could they know how the furniture was placed in the rooms, or the colors of the houses unless they were really there? Did the FBI get all that information for them?

Exhibit 10 was the only document not typed on the Hiss typewriter. Chambers showed his honesty when he was asked about it and said, "Perhaps you are right. Exhibit 10 looks like the stuff I got from Harry White." He did not have to change his mind. If he was lying, he could have kept on lying.

One problem you might have is how could a man like Hiss do these things? He's so handsome. Gee, how could he do it? Well, what about Wadleigh? His father was a minister. He was educated in Europe. Hiss went to Harvard and then to Germany and Chicago to study. Both men ended up in the State Department. Don't be fooled by looks. Judge the facts.

Now why did I call Wadleigh as a witness? Because the defense indicated that Wadleigh was the thief, not Hiss. So I called him. And he told you he did not take these documents.

The defense said the documents were stolen by one man. But they cannot explain the last three telegrams in that set that had Hiss's initials on them.

Can you imagine anybody getting past Miss Lincoln into Sayre's office to steal documents? Miss Lincoln said that carbons always accompanied these documents. Anybody who has worked for the government can tell you that there must have been thousands of carbons traveling around with these documents. And Hiss stole many of them.

Now as to the second count. Did Hiss see Chambers after January 1, 1937? The rug seems to prove it right there. And what better proof do you want that

Hiss saw Chambers in 1937 than the $400 loan? And what about the New Year's Eve party on December 31, 1936? Of course the defense tells us that party didn't happen because the Hisses were up in Chappaqua then. They showed a letter written near the end of December 1936. But Dr. Nicholson said, "I saw Timmy on January 2." Mrs. Hiss was back for that New Year's Eve party.

The Hisses say they gave the typewriter to the Catletts in December 1937 because it was a wreck. But when did the Catletts really get the typewriter? When Chambers quit the party in 1938. Because at that time the Hisses realized, Well, we've got the rug stored away. The only other thing that could get us in trouble other than Chambers's word is the typewriter. They knew if they sold the typewriter, it might be traced. If they dropped it off the bridge into the Potomac River, somebody might see them. So what did they do? They gave it to their trusted maid's children, knowing full well that they didn't type and that the typewriter would be abused and gradually disintegrate. But Burnetta Fisher used the typewriter in school and Mr. Feehan from the FBI typed on it without trouble. So why wouldn't Mrs. Hiss let their boy learn to type on it?

We have the secret documents, and the experts agreed they were typed on the Woodstock. So how does Hiss get around that? He says, "Wadleigh did it. X did it. Y did. Anybody but me." Isn't that the action of a coward, who is cornered, pointing frantically and accusing people? This is standard Communist party practice, isn't it? Accuse the other guy, accuse the judge, accuse everybody.

The defense says that somebody wearing overall and a hat with "Woodstock Repair" written on it went to the Catletts. He asks innocent Mrs. Catlett, "I am the repair man. Where is the machine?" Mrs. Catlett asks which machine he wants. He says the Woodstock. She tells him where it is. Then switch to the next scene. It's the middle of one of those dances the Catletts gave. Chambers sneaks into the house, mingles with the dancers, and then types the stuff. Oh, Mr. Cross, you have to do better than that.

And why would Chambers lie? Why should he leave a $30,000 job, accuse Hiss unjustly, and risk his future?

When you go into the jury room, I want you to look at these typewritten documents. I found some common typing errors in the documents. You will also see similar mistakes in them and in letters typed by Mrs. Hiss. You will see the same mistakes on both: The following combinations: r for i, f for g, f for d. Each of the typewritten documents and the handwritten memos has the same message: "Alger Hiss, you were the traitor."

Because of these stolen documents, strictly confidential information was transferred to Russia. That was espionage. The other, more significant damage was that the Russians got our coded cables and got the chance to break our codes.

One of Mr. Hiss's handwritten memos is dated when Wadleigh was on the high seas. Now why did this brilliant fellow make a word-for-word copy of a cable involving a passport fraud when all he had to do was tell Mr. Sayre about trade agreements? Why? Because the telegram was about a Russian informer. We have not heard about that poor fellow since.

And why were all four of these notes neatly folded instead of crumpled? Because that's how Alger Hiss took them out of the office. If a note is no longer of use to you, you just crumple it up and throw it away. You don't go through this business of folding it unless you are going to take it out.

Ladies and gentlemen, what do the microfilm, the memos, and the typewriter prove? Treason, and Hiss is the traitor. Go into the jury room and come back with the courage of your convictions and tell this world that our faith in the American jury system is well founded.

The Judge's Charge

Friday, January 20, 1950

Next Judge Goddard talked to the jury. He *charged* or instructed the jury with the law. He explained how the law applied to this case, and how the jury must follow it in thinking about the case and reaching their verdict. A judge's charge is supposed to be impartial—favoring neither one side nor the other.

You must decide if Mr. Hiss committed perjury—if he willfully gave false testimony while under oath.

There has been much testimony about Mr. Hiss's good character. Evidence of good character may create a reasonable doubt where without such evidence no reasonable doubt would exist. But if the evidence satisfies you beyond a reasonable doubt that the defendant is guilty, you should not acquit him because previously he had a good reputation. Perhaps he did not reveal to his friends his real character or acts.

You decide all questions of fact. You decide the importance and credibility of each witness. Consider a witness's demeanor, background, and frankness or lack of frankness. Consider his accuracy of recollection. Was the witness's testimony supported or contradicted by other testimony? Did the witness have an interest in the outcome of the trial and color his or her testimony or withhold certain facts?

Dr. Binger attacked Mr. Chambers's credibility. He said he has a psychopathic personality. You may accept his opinions about Chambers's mental condition and still find that he told the truth here.

Mr. Chambers is the only witness who has sworn that Mr. Hiss was a spy. To convict Mr. Hiss, you must believe Mr. Chambers's testimony beyond a reasonable doubt *and* find other trustworthy evidence which corroborates that testimony.

To find Mr. Hiss guilty of Count II, you must believe beyond a reasonable doubt that Mr. Chambers saw Mr. Hiss after January 1, 1937, and find trustworthy corroboration of his testimony or believe his wife's testimony. If you do not believe Mr. Chambers, or if you do believe him but do not find other confirming evidence, you must return a verdict of not guilty. You may find the defendant guilty or not guilty on both counts.

Be the Jury

The jury began its deliberations. They had to decide:

- *Did the prosecutor prove Alger Hiss guilty of perjury beyond a reasonable doubt?*

- *Count I: Did Hiss lie when he said he did not pass Chambers these documents dated January–March 1938?*

- *Count II: Did Hiss lie when he said he did not see Chambers after January 1, 1937?*

Go over what each prosecution witness said. Did you believe the witness? Did the cross-examination prove the testimony was false or unreliable?

Go over what each defense witness said. Did you believe the witness? Did the cross-examination prove the testimony was false or unreliable?

When jurors review evidence to determine facts, they may call in the court stenographer to read back testimony and the lawyers' and judge's statements. At any point in your deliberations, you may turn back to clarify the testimony. Use the Stenographer's Notes to locate specific points.

Remember, you may find Hiss guilty or not guilty on both counts.

When you have reached a verdict, turn the page to see what the jury decided.

The Verdict

At 2:47 P.M., on Saturday, January 21, 1950, after twenty-three hours and forty minutes, the jury returned to the courtroom. The clerk called the jurors' names. Then the clerk asked the forelady, Mrs. Alan Condell, "Have you agreed on your verdict?"

"Yes, we have," she answered.

Hiss's face showed no sign of emotion. Neither did his wife's. He touched her folded hands with his right hand and for a second a smile crossed his face. His wife smiled back.

"How say you?" asked the clerk.

"We find the defendant guilty on the first count and guilty on the second count."

The reporters rushed for the door; the spectators talked among themselves. The judge thanked the jury and dismissed them. A half hour later Hiss and his wife wended their way down the courthouse steps through a crowd of photographers and reporters into a car. Someone thrust a microphone into the car, and Hiss said, "I have no comment."

On January 25, 1950, the judge sentenced Hiss to five years in prison for each count—the sentences to run concurrently, or at the same time. Hiss spoke at the sentencing: "I want to say that I am confident that in the future the full facts of how Whittaker Chambers carried out the forgery by typewriter will be disclosed."

HISS IS GUILTY!

Headline from the *New York Journal American*

The Appeals for a New Trial

Hiss did not give up trying to clear his name. He appealed the verdict, asking for a new trial. To get a new trial, lawyers must show that something happened during the trial that violated the defendant's rights or they must produce new evidence that would have affected the verdict.

The first defense motion stated that there was prejudicial conduct by the judge that violated Hiss's rights.

Defense Motion No. 1:

Judge Goddard should not have allowed William Rosen to take the stand. The judge knew beforehand that Rosen would not answer questions. But he was called as a witness anyway. His denials left the jury with the impression that a "possible" Communist had received Hiss's car from Hiss.

The judge should also not have allowed Edith Murray's testimony. She was first produced on the last day of the second trial. She should have been listed as a witness when the prosecution presented its case. Though Chambers testified to a long and close relationship with the Hisses, in public as well as in private, Murray was the only witness who testified to seeing them together. Her last-minute appearance enhanced the dramatic effect on the jury and deprived the defense of time to prepare for a proper cross-examination.

The second motion stated that Prosecutor Murphy's remarks during his opening and closing statements were unfair and prejudicial to Hiss.

Defense Motion No. 2:

In his opening statement the prosecutor said that the grand jury had not believed Hiss and had indicted him. This statement was prejudicial, for it planted the idea that the grand jury thought Hiss was guilty. An indictment is not proof that someone is guilty. Guilt or lack of guilt is decided by a jury.

The prosecutor misled the jury during his closing statement when he repeated the statement that the defendant had lied to the grand jury and that the grand jury believed Chambers.

The prosecutor played upon the prejudices of the times. He exploited the fear of communism. In his closing he said that Hiss had used "standard Communist party practice. Accuse the other guy, accuse the judge, accuse everybody." He used this same unfair tactic when he took the defense's statement that certain FBI practices were "overzealous" and said: "This is open season on the FBI. Everybody is taking potshots at them. That's the Communist party line."

It was improper that during the closing statement he told the jury that he "had noticed some common typing errors" that they might look at, too. The jury can only consider evidence introduced in the court. The prosecutor's observations had not been given in evidence. There was no chance for the defense to answer these charges.

The third motion questioned the authenticity of the Woodstock typewriter; the defense believed the typewriter was a crucial factor in the conviction of Hiss.

Defense Motion No. 3

The verdict was based in large part on the fact that the Hiss typewriter had been used to type the documents. But newly discovered evidence strongly suggested that this typewriter was a carefully constructed substitute, which could only have been made for the deliberate purpose of falsely incriminating Alger Hiss.

The defense produced two affidavits to show that the Woodstock typewriter might not have been Hiss's machine.

Marty K. Tytell, a typewriter engineer, without ever seeing the Woodstock, worked from the sample documents and built a machine that duplicated the ten or so characters that FBI agent Feehan said proved that the documents had been typed on Hiss's Woodstock.

Elizabeth McCarthy, a documents expert, examined samples from both typewriters. She concluded that experts would have great difficulty distinguishing samples from Tytell's machine from samples typed on the Woodstock. She studied Feehan's testimony, and she concluded that if a document expert applied Feehan's standard to specimens from both machines, the expert would conclude that a single machine had been used to type both sets.

The judge turned down all of Hiss's motions for a new trial. Hiss appealed to the court of appeals. A panel of three judges turned down the appeal.

Hiss appealed to the United States Supreme Court, the highest court in the land, to review the case. The justices voted 4 to 2 against hearing the case. Justices Frankfurter and Reed disqualified themselves from the decision because they had been character witnesses for Hiss at the trial. Justice Tom Clark disqualified himself because he had been Attorney General when Hiss was indicted.

What Happened to Alger Hiss?

On March 22, 1951, Hiss went to prison. He spent forty-four months in a federal penitentiary. Priscilla got a job in a bookstore and brought up their ten-year-old son, Anthony. Hiss was freed on Friday, November 26, 1954. He spent the next sixteen months writing a book, *In the Court of Public Opinion*, in which he analyzed why the evidence at his trial was insufficient to convict him of perjury. Then he found a job working as an assistant to the president of a small company that produced novelty costume jewelry.

In 1959 he and Priscilla separated. At the same time, he lost his job. He found work as a salesman of office supplies and printing and began rebuilding his life. He remarried. He became a frequent speaker at colleges and universities about his years in government service and his case. There is now an endowed professorship at Bard College, in Annandale-on-Hudson, New York, called the Alger Hiss Chair. He was eventually readmitted to the Massachusetts bar.

The Final Petition

In 1974, under the Freedom of Information Act, Hiss secured copies of FBI and Department of Justice files about him. In October 1978 he petitioned the court to set aside his conviction for perjury. The petition stated that the government had engaged in serious misconduct that deprived Hiss of a fair trial. New evidence from the files explained why the trial had been unfair.

The prosecution used an informer within the defense.

Horace Schmahl was a private investigator employed by the defense from October 1948 to early 1949. During this time and after, he met repeatedly with the FBI agents and Prosecutor Murphy. He told them what the defense was doing and planning. This deprived Hiss of the assistance of counsel guaranteed under the Sixth Amendment.

The prosecution conspired to conceal important statements by Chambers to the FBI.

At both trials Chambers said that he got $400 from Hiss. But in an earlier FBI interview, he said he borrowed $500 from Hiss. We believe that between the date Chambers told this to the FBI and the first trial, he discovered that the Hisses had withdrawn $400 from their bank account in November 1937. So he changed his story. This early FBI interview was never given to the defense, as is required by federal law.

The government also concealed evidence relating to the date on which Chambers left the Communist party, a crucial issue in the case.

The prosecution made serious misrepresentations to the judge, jury, and defense.

The government submitted the Woodstock typewriter as having once belonged to the Hisses and having typed the documents. But FBI files reveal that, during the first trial, the prosecution knew that the Woodstock could not have been the Hiss typewriter. The government concealed this evidence and deliberately misled the court by making the Woodstock an important part of its case. When the defense later appealed the verdict and challenged the typewriter's authenticity, the government again misled the court and defense. The serial number on the Woodstock was 230,099. The Hiss typewriter was bought in 1927. FBI memos show that the serial number of a typewriter bought in 1927 would have been less than 177,000. So the Woodstock exhibit was not manufactured until late August 1929, and therefore could not have typed Mrs. Hiss's letters dated July 1929.

The prosecution coached an important witness.

Edith Murray's testimony was a bombshell, coming at the very end of the trial. She was the only person, other than the Chamberses, to say that the two couples had been together. Her pretrial testimony, which was not made available to the defense before she took the stand, shows that an FBI agent showed her a photograph and told her it was a woman named Priscilla Hiss.

This is not the way Mrs. Murray described the conversation when she gave her testimony. At the trial she said she identified the Hisses in the courthouse hall. She looked around and couldn't find anybody that she knew. Then she saw Mr. and Mrs. Hiss come over, "and right away I knew them." When taken with her preparation (being shown the photographs and told the names of the people), it is difficult to conceive of a less reliable method of securing an identification.

Hiss's petition was turned down. But he continued to be optimistic that his innocence would be revealed someday.

What Happened to Whittaker Chambers?

Chambers lost his job; his publisher at *Time* thought he was too controversial to be associated with the magazine. He went back to his farm in Maryland and worked on his autobiography, *Witness*. It became a best-seller when it was published in 1952. Shortly after publication, he suffered his third heart attack. In 1957 he got a job on the *National Review*, an anticommunist, conservative political magazine. His health continued to deteriorate, and in 1958 he had another heart attack. Two years later he resigned from the *National Review*. On July 9, 1961, he suffered another heart attack and died. Posthumously Chambers received the Medal of Freedom, the highest civilian honor, from President Ronald Reagan. His farm was designated a National Historic Landmark.

Guilty or Innocent?

For more than forty years, Alger Hiss has professed his innocence.

On October 15, 1992, Colonel General Dmitri Antonovich Volkogonov, historian and military counselor to Russian President Boris Yeltsin, and head of the Supreme Council commission on the K.G.B and military-intelligence archives of the former Soviet Union, appeared on television. His press conference was broadcast live around the world.

Volkogonov stated that a careful review of a

"huge amount of documents" had led him to "make a firm conclusion that Alger Hiss was not ever or anywhere recruited as an agent of the intelligence services of the Soviet Union. "

He also said that Soviet archives revealed that Chambers had never had "any kind of secret or spy information." "Tell Alger Hiss that the heavy weight should be lifted from his heart. May he in his advanced age breathe freely and look with wide-open eyes at this wonderful, complex, and multifaceted world of ours."

Some critics of Hiss questioned how thorough Volkogonov's search through the millions of pages of material in Soviet archives was. But eighty-seven-year-old Alger Hiss celebrated the good news with his family and friends.

What Do You Think?

If Alger Hiss didn't steal the documents, who did?
Why did they do it, and how was it done?

Author's Note

The testimony in this book was edited from the transcript of the trial. The descriptions of people and interactions in the courtroom were taken from newspaper articles. For purposes of space, questions and answers were often combined. Not all witness evidence was included in this book, nor were all the days of the trial. But the most important facts and contradictions have been included to give a balanced picture so that you could be a fair juror.

Acknowledgments

I thank Alan H. Levine, who took time from his busy teaching schedule and from his commitment to providing legal protection to all Americans to read this manuscript. Michael Donlon, Angelica Gomez, Melony Lopez, Srsti Purcell, Michael Reilly, and Sydney Seifert of Elaine Shapiro's fifth grade class at P.S. 199 in New York City were thoughtful and insightful critics of this book. The New York Public Library provided space in the Wertheim Study to facilitate my research, and the library staff, as always, proved tireless in answering all requests. Judith Mellins at the Harvard Law School Library graciously smoothed my entry into the Alger Hiss Papers. Ari, Micki, and Sid Handel provided humor, food, lodgings, and favors during my Boston stay with them. Michele Drohan dug up essential photographs and newspaper clippings. A special thanks to Katherine Brown Tegen and Renée Cafiero, who always help me clean up my act.

Bibliography

Chambers, Whittaker. *Witness*. New York: Random House, *.he Court of Public Opinion*. New York: Knopf, 1957.

Jowitt, William Allen. *The Strange Case of Alger Hiss*. Garden City, New York: Doubleday, 1953.

Smith, John Chabot. *Alger Hiss: The True Story*. New York: Penguin Books, 1977.

Tiger, Edith, ed., *In Re Alger Hiss: Petition for a Writ of Error*, New York: Hill and Wang, 1979.

United States of America against Alger Hiss. Transcript of Record . . . Appeal from the District Court of the United States for the Southern District of New York, Volumes I–X. Sayre, Pennsylvania: Murrelle Printing Company, 1950.

Weinstein, Allen. *Perjury: The Hiss-Chambers Case*. New York: Knopf, 1978.

Newspapers consulted were *The New York Times* and the *New York Herald Tribune*.

Stenographer's Notes

These notes cover only testimony accepted at the trial because that is all you, as jury members, are allowed to see.

Page numbers in *italics* refer to illustrations.

Doreen Rappaport

is the author of many books for children, including three other books in the *Be the Judge • Be the Jury* series: THE LIZZIE BORDEN TRIAL, THE SACCO-VANZETTI TRIAL, and TINKER VS. DES MOINES: *Student Rights on Trial;* LIVING DANGEROUSLY: *American Women Who Risked Their Lives for Adventure;* ESCAPE FROM SLAVERY: *Five Journeys to Freedom,* a 1991 Notable Children's Trade Book in the Field of Social Studies (NCSS/CBC); THE BOSTON COFFEE PARTY; TROUBLE AT THE MINES, an Honor Book for the 1988 Jane Addams Children's Book Award; and AMERICAN WOMEN: *Their Lives in Their Words,* a 1990 Notable Children's Trade Book in the Field of Social Studies (NCSS/CBC) and a 1992 ALA Best Book for Young Adults.

Ms. Rappaport lives in New York City. When she is not writing, she is dreaming about traveling or hip-hop dancing.